Verge 2025

Verge 2025

Blue

Edited by
Cassie Kropp, Yong Li,
Adara Rose Luis and Jonathan Ricketson

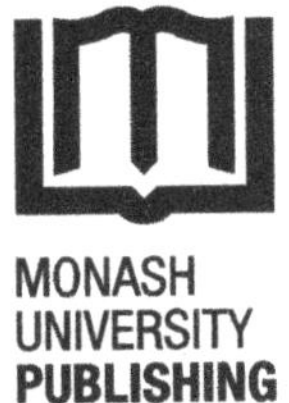

Published by Monash University Publishing

Matheson Library Annexe
40 Exhibition Walk
Monash University
Clayton, Victoria 3800, Australia
publishing.monash.edu/

Monash University Publishing: the discussion starts here

Verge 2025: Blue
ISBN: 9781923192485 (paperback)
ISBN: 9781923192492 (PDF)
ISBN: 9781923192508 (ePub)
ISSN: 2208-5637

Design by Les Thomas
Typesetting by Jo Mullins

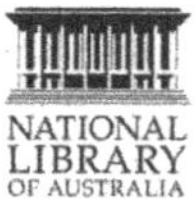

A catalogue record for this book is available from the National Library of Australia

Printed in Australia by Griffin Press

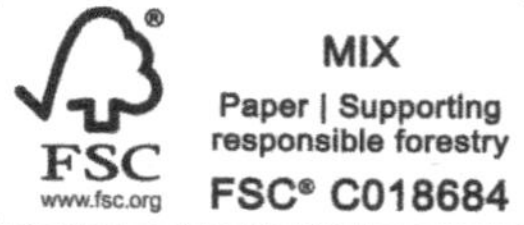

The paper this book is printed on is certified against the Forest Stewardship Council® Standards. Griffin Press holds chain of custody certification SCS-COC-001185. FSC® promotes environmentally responsible, socially beneficial and economically viable management of the world's forests.

Contents

About the Editors

Cassie Kropp (they/she) is studying a Masters of Research in Languages, Literatures, Cultures and Linguistics at Monash University. Their plays have been performed in the Anywhere Theatre Festival in Brisbane but now they focus more on academic writing.

Yong Li holds a bachelor's degree and a PhD from Zhejiang University in Hangzhou, China. She is a lecturer in the School of Marxism at Shanghai Maritime University and a visiting scholar in Chinese Studies at Monash University. Her recent publications appear in *Waste Management*, *Journal of Environmental Management* and *Environmental Research Communications*, among others. Her research interests encompass pro-environmental psychology and behaviour, political trust and NPO management.

Adara Rose Luis is a writer, scholar and poet. Her research examines male violence against girls and women in children's and young adult literature. Adara has presented at international conferences and published poetry, and has held academic editing roles.

Jonathan Ricketson is completing a PhD in Creative Writing at Monash University. His fiction and nonfiction writing has been published in *Meanjin*, *Australian Book Review* and *Griffith Review*. He is the 2025 *ABR* Rising Star.

Introduction

This year's *Verge* theme was inspired by Maggie Nelson's groundbreaking work of prose-poetry, *Bluets* (2009). She opens the collection musing: 'Suppose I were to begin by saying that I had fallen in love with a color.'

Blue is the most mysterious and evocative of colours. It can signify the beginning of love and the end of life, tranquillity and tension, the fluid and the fixed. In the current edition of *Verge*, fifty-three contributors share responses to blue that span fiction, nonfiction, poetry and experimental forms.

In some of the prose pieces, blue signifies transformation and transcendence. In Joshua Klarica's 'Prompt', blue represents the brave new world of artificial intelligence, and the shifting relationship between a chatbot, its designers and a disillusioned user. Elena Disilvestro's 'Vessel' is a work in the body horror genre, utilising blue to explore the liminality between the physical and spiritual realms. Blue is metaphorical in Suzanne Hermanocz's 'The Spirit of Blue', which is focused on the psychology of men at different stages of life. In Bill Collopy's 'Infinity Dancing', the past and present blur together, with blue echoing in the lingering, punishing effects of trauma.

Many poetic works in the collection capture the synaesthetic qualities of blue, experimenting with the use of sound and movement. There is blue in the decibels of tree cricks hatching in Mark O'Flynn's 'Cicadas'; blue in the tonal percussion of the humpback whale song in Scott-Patrick Mitchell's 'Blue Whale Watching'; blue in the movement of swallows in Sharon Kernot's 'Wetland Walk', filling the sky with circles and figure eights. Blue can also be suggestive of atmosphere and place, transporting readers all around the globe, taking us from the bush to the wilds of the ocean, from Pakistan to the streets of Paris.

The elasticity of this year's theme has yielded an astonishing breadth of responses, from the intensely personal to the global and to the infinite. They testify to the many ways in which a colour can infiltrate our lives, inside and out. Blue is an emotional state; it is the natural environment and technology; it is past, present and future.

Jonathan Ricketson, Co-Editor

1

Full-Time at the Poetry Factory

Allan Lake

No watch (and clock on the wall
has a flat battery), so poet wouldn't
know the time, other than coffee
and toast o'clock. Block-out curtains
soften the difference between day/night.
The Muse can make demands at any
moment, but poets must doze sometimes
and send submissions, like invoices,
which should be called outvoices.
Day of the week (or month) is guesswork
that lacks weight, unless poet waits
for the result of a poetry competition
which was entered in a fleeting moment
of self-confidence or hallucination.
Pay is much less than minimal, so
how to survive? It is not so much
frugality; there simply is no desire
to shop. Poets are too preoccupied
with the latest (lame) poem that needs
a series of operations to correct this,
amputate that. It's life in *slowmo*:
staring toward (but not at) the robin's egg blue wall,
pecking at keys, scribbling notes
to self with 'borrowed' pens.
Now and then poets venture outside
for supplies or poetry prompts,

to check changing climate,
to confirm that civilisation,
that creative/destructive process,
has not collapsed for want
of an excellent poem—
not   quite   yet.

2

Blue History

Kate O'Neil

After the pencilled scribbles of infancy
where anything was possible,
came the responsibility of blue ink,
the discipline of copperplate.

The school supplied slope cards
to ensure the correct *s l a n t.*

Though prone to blots and smudges,
and difficult to erase,
ink assumed Authority,
the stamp of permanence.

It dyed the blank white of new pages
with the stain of words,
chosen by someone,
sometime,
somewhere,
becoming in time the records
for age after age,
indelibly blue.

Margins were an exception—
to be ruled in erasable pencil only.

3

Blue and Yellow Friendship

Aries M. Gacutan

hello, golden world!
i am thinking about how
blue speaks glowingly to yellow—
how the night sky talks
          to window talks to bird in tree
          talks to puddle of streetlight
how the conversation of cars
is etched in their blurred silhouettes

how the saffron trills against
the cadmium blue
defies the axial tilt
          speaking cool breeze in summertime
          speaking bright shower and winter rain

i see   globules of sunlight
          dripping down
          greyblue tree trunks
in tribute, i spoon honey
          into an aegean mug

when friends speak
          it is in swirls of slate and goldenrod
i am propping myself up
          an attentive house   on stilts

and from up here you could touch
the whole of it
            tracing the warm line of rainbows
            left on the bathroom floor

4

Montmartre Mirror

Will Hunt

He is drawing me as I write him, refracted.
The sunlight half-glows; me in half,
profile, the shaded side to his seat
across the Montmartre square, voyeuristic
tourism where we have exchanged art:
opal cascades of poetry, painting, pausing.

He sits on a sunlit bench, with only a black
fineliner and a tattered journal. Ink, not granite,
to steal me in this light, here as I am,
physicality and all. He squints through me,
draws through me, erasing the asides.

He moves, a different angle, perhaps
a different light. My beard is patched:
my book damaged but new—
black-tarred from the tote bag
capturing—with a flash—a blemished
and worn English translation of *War*, a mirror
into Céline, a man, a modernist, a horror.

The Basilica of the Sacré Cœur hangs,
yesterday scratched against the wind, today
the blue, Picasso sky-crystal. I do not
have time to see it, not the patience—
the scammers scratch at my arms,
pulling me down with bracelets:
'Where are you from, sir? Sir!'

I wave them away and witness:
the Parisian lie.

5

New Year's Day, Auckland, 1969

Stephen Smithyman

The year begins in rain. Rain on the city,
rain on the quiet streets, rain on the deserted parks,
rain on the bronze and birdshit-streaked statue
of Queen Victoria, where she stands in Albert Park,
opposite the white 'wedding cake' clock tower
of Auckland University. The rain has washed
the city clean—clean like tears, clean like
baptismal water with its promise of new life.
A new life! That's what the young man wants,
skulking in his childhood bedroom—a child
no more—acutely aware of the mess he has made
of his life, the ever present sense of failure
that follows him around like a faithful dog at heel.
He failed at school. He dropped out of university.
Now he hides in his bedroom, uncertain where else
he can go or what the inscrutable future holds for him.
Slender evidence of his life surrounds him, a drawing
of a dead bird, a poem to a girl he once loved, pinned
on the wall. He can hear his parents, quarrelling
in the kitchen. This is the sound of his childhood—
his parents' incessant bickering, rising to a scream,
followed by tears and silence, against a background
of his mother's worsening illness, his father's
increasing drinking. When he thinks about it,
all he sees is black, that blackness closing in
around him like the winter his mother talked about,
which never goes away, like the sound of that rain
falling everywhere, dampening last night's celebrations,

extinguishing the fires and rockets, muting the sirens,
and then again, this morning, washing the city clean,
holding out its fragile promise of forgetting, its distant
possibility of forgiveness, of renewal, the perpetually
mourning bride stepping up to the wedding cake
once more...like the sound of that New Year's rain.

6

Καημός (Kaimós)

Amelia Theodorakis

I understand now what a room can do to a body,
to a spirit, the shape of fossils changes when turned
in the hand too long, I saw myself with water, felt
compelled to rest my feet in the sea's grass, the more
glory to sway in with the hips, you need a bigger
hill to die on though and a string quartet to go
down with, I remember how we bumped blue
bodies, rubbed lips 'til they bled, imagine if you
had wanted the crown of my head cupped in your
hand for centuries, my body and all its determined
salt, in the ancient stone burial chamber of four in
the morning, I ran my hands along the splitting
geology of an hour and wondered whether I
would be the cat or the Egyptian in the next life,
gloriously hooked out of myself through the nasal
canal, embalmed in olive oil and old air, to be
admired in glittering expiry for a thousand years,
but who am I to deserve such eternity, the heart
feels absence like an ultraviolence, yours was an
electrical charge flashing right through mine,
by then it was only a matter of draining the blood
weight, the heartbeat of everything is to become
utterly self-scarred but it's a human distraction
to fetter and yoke what resists, one thing I didn't say,
blistering in my revenge dress on your sandstone
doorstep, you framed by light, the only time I saw
you look like the word surrender. I was tired of being
held in the fluid of things I could not submit.

7

In the Vicinity of a Love Poem

Steve Evans

If you write a love poem, she said,
never mention love.

So, when she pauses at the mirror
with that blue as irises' blue in her eyes,
or her fingers unexpectedly brush my skin,
or she leaves the porch light on for me when I'm late,
or her hand seeks mine in a lift,
or she makes that little seismic twitch in her sleep—
anything from the whole album,
the whole fistful of metaphors
amounting to one simple-as-the-simplest thing
stitched loosely to the next
I might write it down
but without a hint of the taboo word,
having no need
since every love poem has her in it.

8

Blue Geometries

for Clare

Hannah McCann

Train doors close   tonight I caught you up
          a year's worth of mistakes
taking breaks from my life   like kicking bareback
flanks   how I've trampled over
          all my daisy blessings   as usual
                    falling off good habits
again and again   *today my car unlocked itself*
          started windscreen wiping
on the highway   some ghost in my machine
          the shape of our friendship   the way
a cutter presses into dough   leaves a gap
     my phone loses reception in the tunnel
          across the aisle   three passengers swap
stories   *worst ever memories*
  a horse pulling someone into barbed wire   a blood
leech in the bed   a sister gripping the soft body
of a mouse   the friends depart
                the seats are blue geometries
strips of light overhead   like an emergency path
          I manage to load an article
can tech become better   *at humanity than we are*
                a person rests their head
on someone's shoulder   there is so much intimacy
          in this space   an aching cough
at the window   strange knees near my bare legs
                two pink press-on nails skittering the floor
          I would message to say I miss you
but the signal

9

Blue

Keren Heenan

She takes a step back from the canvas. Blue stares back and is meaningless, still. Something needs to show itself—a layer, an expression of the emptiness in her chest. The old dog, Penny, staggers to her feet, falls as she tries to shake herself, then stumbles over to Eva, rests her head against her knee as if to console or encourage.

Lawrence appears at the door, glances at the canvas and raises his eyebrows. 'There are other colours you know.' As he walks away, he says over his shoulder, 'I need a lift to the pub soon, remember? It's Friday. Jed'll give me a lift home.' Eva hears the newspaper shaken out, chair scraping on the tiles. He calls out, 'Hey, did you know,' and she closes her eyes, waiting, 'that the Earth looks blue from out in space?'

'Yes, I did know that. I've always known that.' She opens her eyes and focuses on the blue paint, the swirl of aquamarine into something paler, more mint than blue.

'Well, you couldn't always have known it, like, literally. I can just see you calling from your cot—*I say, the Earth looks blue from space*,' and he cracks the air with his laughter. 'You were one hell of a *clever* baby.'

Once, she could have laughed along with him. But there's an edge now that feels sharp, unfamiliar. She blocks out his mutterings and self-appreciative bursts of laughter. Works a more intense cobalt blue onto the canvas in a flurry of swirls. Stepping back from the canvas, she thinks that he has probably just pointed out a failing; hers, not his.

Eva ruffles Penny's ears and leads her back to the cushion in the corner. 'I'll be back soon, Pen,' she says.

Out in the kitchen Lawrence is flipping through the newspaper, pretending not to look impatient. He glances up, 'You ready?'

She nods, grabs the keys. It's only a five-minute drive. She wonders why he doesn't walk but has given up asking. Usually, Jed picks him up. There's no sharing of the onus of driving. It's just accepted that Lawrence will get drunk and the others know when to stop. It wasn't always like that. The old Laurie would've taken his turn at being the sober driver. 'Poor old Lozza,' she'd overheard Jed one night at a barbeque. 'He's got a lot on his plate. I don't mind being the designated driver come Fridays.' And she'd thought about that *lot on his plate*. Knew it probably included her. Wondered what Lawrence says about her when he's drunk, even when he's not drunk. His words to her: 'You've got to move on, you can't do that if you keep bringing it up.' *It*. Not even *him*, but *it*.

She parks in the car park, Lawrence leans across and his dry lips brush her cheek. 'See ya. I'll try not to get too stonkered,' he says.

'Sure.' She lifts her finger in a wave. He shuts the door, runs his hand through his hair and heads to the beer garden. She likes Fridays. Does not accept invitations for anything on a Friday. Invites herself to stay home: paint, not paint, weep, not weep, drink wine, walk, wonder what else there is.

Back home, Penny whimpers with excitement behind the screen door. Shuffles back as Eva comes in. 'Come on, Pen, just us girls now.' She fills the dog bowl with dry snacks, watches Penny wolf them down. She pours a glass of wine and goes to the back room. Stands at the door a moment looking at the canvas, sips the wine. Penny pushes past Eva's legs, flops on the cushion, head on paws.

Tonight, when Lawrence comes home, he will be slurring and stumbling and his beer breath will be intolerable. He'll come crashing into the bedroom, waking her as he undresses, overbalancing on one foot, pulling off trousers or socks. She will have to ask him to sleep in the spare room. Once, his head had struck the corner of the bed, and she'd had to get up then, stop the bleeding, give some form of sympathy. She used to find him amusing when he was like this—loveably clumsy. But that was before it became every Friday night.

Eva squints towards the canvas, trying to see with blurred vision, hoping for a sense of satisfaction but feeling only disappointment. She sees nothing new. It's as if she is painting the same thing over and over. She knows that is what she is doing. Painting all in blue now: indigo, azure, a blue as delicately pale as starling eggs, cerulean, lapis lazuli. She used to feel still and whole when blue covered the canvas; her palette knife chunking the paint into crests of colour, blending one into the other. Bleeding blue. But now, it is as if she is simply covering a surface. Nothing moves inside her.

Out the window the sky is grey but there are chinks of blue here and there, waiting to peek through. She leaves the wine, takes her jacket from the back of the chair. 'Come on, Pen, a drive. That's what we need, maybe a walk for me.'

Eva has to lift Penny into the back seat. The old dog looks at her as if she's unsure, like she might be going to the vet—usually the only time she gets a ride these days. 'It's okay, Penny, we're just going for a drive.'

Out along the road she opens the window, her hair blows across her face. She pushes her sunglasses up onto her head so she can see the road. She has the wildest feeling that she could just keep driving, no destination. She turns down the road that leads to the water. Not a swimming beach but cliffs overlooking the relentless waves belting the rocks in a frenzy of white froth. She pulls into the viewing bay, turns off the motor and sits staring out at the far horizon. When she comes here, she likes to sit a while and watch that flat, calm blue line. She knows the deceit of distance though. That Earth is not really blue. That out there in the ocean it would be cold and deep and wild. But here in the car, she can drift in a warm, quiet spell. Feel the spirit level in her chest tilt to balance. She's aware of the churn of water beneath her against the rocks, can hear its rush and crash. Keeps her eyes on the still and steady line.

Penny clambers to her feet, reminding Eva that she is there. Eva reaches around and rests one hand on her head, ruffles her ears. 'I know, Penny, we'll get going.'

Rain starts to patter against the window, building to a steady downpour. A walk is not such an enjoyable prospect now. She drives home, wipers beating a steady tattoo and Penny's hot meaty breath fogging the inside of the windows.

When she gets up the next morning, she hears snoring from behind the closed door of the spare room. In the kitchen on the cold tiled floor, Penny is disturbingly still. Eva drops to her knees, reaches out slowly and places one hand on the old dog's flank, and she knows. Crouches on the floor beside her and stays that way crying until Lawrence comes bleary-eyed into the kitchen. 'What're you doing?'

They bury Penny in the garden, in the only soft earth they can find near the compost bin. Eva moves a pot of lavender and a rock to the site. Lawrence starts the mower and cuts swathes through grass that does not need mowing, bending to pull at weeds along the path. She watches his bent form, his concentrated gaze. Turns and walks inside.

She goes to the back room, squeezes black and blue directly onto the canvas, covering the ridges of colour from before. A blue that is as black as black without being wholly black. Works them together, scraping and rasping across the surface until she bends forward and rests her forehead on the canvas. Stabs the palette knife into the canvas, again, and again, throws it to the floor.

'I'm going for a drive,' she calls from the back door. Lawrence looks up, nods, though he couldn't possibly hear her over the mower. He straightens, points to his forehead then to Eva. She runs the back of her wrist over her forehead, it comes away black-blue. She nods, goes inside and washes it off.

Out on the road she passes the turn-off to the cliffs. There's a bay further around the heads where swimming is possible. She parks and takes her towel, heads down the steps to the sand. Prickly mimosa sighs alongside her in the breeze.

The beach is deserted. Exactly how she likes it: water, sky and sand, that one rock away to the right like a giant turtle awaiting arrivals from the sea. She drops her towel, takes her dress off and walks to the water, curling her toes into sand. The wind is cool, blowing from the south; her skin prickles into gooseflesh as she anticipates the water's touch.

When she dives in, her skin zings with the chill and liveness of it. She surfaces, swims further out, then flips onto her back in a float. Cirrus scuds the sky above, mounds of cumulus float and patches of blue widen between the clouds. Here, she knows vulnerability, and how easy it would be to just keep swimming—out to the horizon, that ever-changing line, *out to China* where her father had once said she and her kickboard would end up if she kept going. Out and onwards until she could swim no more. Then, how easy to just give yourself up to the deep wild blue.

She kicks herself upright, looks back to the shore. She has floated a long way out, further than she'd thought. She dips forward, kicks and takes a couple of strokes, feeling the pull back towards the horizon. The strength of it like hands tugging her backwards, into where it's green and dark and billowing under a glowering sky. She kicks away, against the invisible hands holding her. Stops when the effort becomes easier, and she dares to look up. The beach is there, close enough now, and she turns into a float again, closes her eyes until her breath is steady.

Held as if by a cupped hand, she watches the drift of clouds above. Here, she can remember, safely. She can be all grief, formless and blind—cry, slap the water or scream and no one will mind. Hear even. No longer the name, he is just a feeling now: a memory of almost weightlessness, compact roundness, of skin and warmth, and the smell of him never leaves her. Her hands rise from the surface, curving around emptiness. The movement unbalances her and she kicks upright a moment, treading water, hands sculling, then back into a float. Not even Penny now to wrap her arms around. Instead, there's a newly turned patch of dirt in the yard to remind of absences—the older one still fresh enough to be raw, unassimilated. This recent one, unable to be hefted without the other clinging, squeezing at her heart. And Lawrence, mowing the grass, silent, bent to the task like it's of the utmost importance.

She feels the cupped hand of the sea again, holding her afloat. Ears just below the surface, she hears the hum and roar of activity far below the seabed, and far beyond the horizon, out into the deep, dark sea. She imagines the grinding, writhing din, the crash and clamour that should be heard across the planet as currents move tirelessly, tectonic plates shift, and on the sea-floor waves thump. But she knows it is all just a hum, beyond human hearing. She imagines it is this hum she has been trying to paint. Something that makes her feel part of a whole again. She closes her eyes; the liquid velvet of the water caresses her skin. A sudden warmth on her eyelids, and she opens her eyes to a patch of blue above her where the clouds have dispersed. If that hum of the world could be a colour, she thinks it would be blue.

At home again, in the backyard, she stands looking at the turned earth, the rock and the flowerpot. Lawrence is in the shed, she can hear him dragging heavy objects, stacking things, tossing junk into a bin. He comes out with the bin, puts it down outside the door. He looks over at her, and something passes between them, a ripple, an echo of the way they'd once been. Then he clamps his jaw, turns away.

She lifts her head to a scrap of blue above, watches the clouds move, the blue widen. Feels the hum softly in her throat as she turns and walks inside.

10

Infinity Dancing

Bill Collopy

By now I know its rhythms. Though starting in the gut as little more than pins and needles, my intruder surges, attacking the chest. Have I timed the painkillers right? If not, agony will blind me to the point of passing out.

Everyone's an expert. But nobody can share this. I hide in a room where the toilet bowl swirls a chlorine blue, proof of cleanliness. I tell a child knocking on the door: ~ Won't be a minute. ~

Traversing an urban sprawl to my brother's home, where windows face an ultramarine bay, and rooftops sport solar panels, I've sipped polite beers until I need this chamber.

~ Don't touch the bottom… ~

My nephew stops carving to smile at old superstitions, from when he was little, in boy colours. An engineer now, he resumes, bisecting the word Birthday.

~ Want a top up? ~

As I decline, my eldest brother pretends not to mind. Others take up the tune.: ~ …which nobody can deny… ~

I frame a sequence of both brothers singing with me at a rare win, before the merger. I can place them either side of me in wedding photos, kept in an indigo album between other records. Who opens them anymore? Who even turns pages? I'm one of the few to keep buying books. Too many, according to my wife. They do not give her joy. What she calls clutter, I call treasure. Our study strains to hold the weight of pages, likewise our corridors and garage. Libby venerates empty surfaces; I see IKEA minimalism, no soul. I can't bear to throw out books. When I'm gone, the family can purge. Libby may sell up. The house will be grabbed by a developer to demolish for units. Town houses will replace history, in catalogue homes not built to last.

My daughters may baulk at chucking out photo albums, but they will consign old essays and maps to recycling, with comics unworthy of a collector's trouble. So, why can't I break the habit of giving books? Neither of my brothers is a reader, nor my children. They have apps. Why impose print on them? Is my laughter bubbling from deep down, a bitter reflux that burns?

Invisible in the cracks, I find a safe place to smile. No one would understand, except maybe Ricky.

My nieces and nephews are now parents. At their children's age, I believed that if I read enough, I could catch up. Other kids seemed to know more. I scanned pages, eyebrows bending with strain, hunting down meanings that I felt lurked just out of sight.

Leaving school, I joined the bank, still reading. Smarter friends were already losing touch with books, plunging into vocational reading. I clung to fantasy, crime, history, philosophy, with a compulsion to acquire knowledge for no purpose. Today my shelves bulge with decades of Popular Science and Newsweek, time-capsules for Nixon, Vietnam, Gorbachev, Hawke and Peacock, and AIDS. Collections of political essays, copies of Punch. And yet I make a living from numbers. I'm still with the same bank. Despite a senior-sounding title I'm barely middle management. I keep expecting them to give me thirty minutes to clean out my things. A few heads rolled after the Royal Commission, but most executives sighed with relief. We have altered our Wedgewood coloured logo twice, and our byzantine mission statement several times. I still count other people's money. Governments rise and fall but I keep the faith, as I stayed true to my team, until the merger. A hand signed the paper. This hybrid club is nothing to me, no matter how many premierships they claim.

The specialist is about my age, perhaps planning for retirement. During my first visit, I examined certificates and degrees on his wall, with photos of daughters in turquoise blazers. He reassured me with talk I couldn't follow. Then the phrase 'hopefully not malignant'. After that, I heard nothing. Lips flapped but only white noise came out. It was the anti-smoking poster that finished me. Cigarettes could kill. A detonation inside, laughter dark as a cave. Nobody else would hear. They never have.

In the small hours I lie twitching. Libby stirs.

~ Are you awake? ~

~ I'm fine. ~

~ Been to the toilet again? ~

~ Go back to sleep. ~

~ You should take one of those pills. ~

~ I have. Go back to sleep. ~

Still an attractive woman, Libby runs her own business. She goes to a gym every second day. She watches what she eats: never anything with mould. She can do better.

Through windows of my brother's house, I see a delftware sky. No retirement lifestyle for me. Tomorrow I'm back at work, following a decimal point through ledgers. Colleagues don't know my trick. Stare hard enough and the numbers writhe like earthworms. Not a joke to share. Instead, I'll overhear staff flirting and making blue jokes. I'll hear bus brakes hiss outside. If I venture out, I might bump into him again, the homeless guy who looks like Krishna. Does he follow me, or have I just started to notice?

On my desk a date will throb from the screen, counting down. I must not wet my face, in case General Dreedle notices, or Colonel Cathcart. Neither of them has a clue. Dreedle would say, coming over:

~ Anything the matter…? ~

Ricky would understand. It's years since I said his name aloud.

In the toilet room, agony unseams me from the nave to the chops. There's a gap where my face should be. From beyond, I hear weight variations in footfall. My brother's grandchildren. Noise cuts a generation knife. I plead for distraction. Anything will do, even prayer.

Spelling bees. Chalkboards. Elbows livid from British Bulldogs in a sheltershed. Knuckles sore from slingshot recoil. Nostrils prick with a perfume of bubble-gum strips, bought from a milk bar, with five cents worth of mixed lollies. What does five cents buy these days? And what's a milk bar?

Nuns loom, bearing the names of male saints, doling out discipline with a bamboo feather duster. I smart from Chinese Burns inflicted by Damien Donleavy or Marco Dorevitch: twin nemeses in Grade One. Damien is a County Court judge now. Marco is a road statistic.

With knees raw from genuflection, I lean in Mass: a hypotenuse, sum of two sides fighting the triangle of want, denial and duty. In class, boy-girl pairs occupy desks. On asphalt we stomp to brass band recordings: single file, left-right-left-right, marching for Christ. A pecking order of bell monitors, chalk monitors and milk monitors, I suffer love pangs: teased by Mary O'Connell while I pine for Anna Vandenberg. Where are they all? If I flip open an album, I'll find my face among classmates or squeezed into the footy team with folded arms. At morning assembly, we drink milk from small bottles. We stand to attention at the sound of a bell. I have no clue how funny we look, until later, when Ricky explains.

In the toilet room, I bite on a scream till I'm blue. If I push enough, the rictus might crush itself into a smirk. Too soon to emerge.

In winter we shiver down to our chilblains, clutching semi-frozen milk. We sing the national anthem to an absent monarch. We chant a prayer for the Pope. In religion class I shuffle holy cards of Our Lady. Finally, the bell.

At home I switch on afternoon cartoons. Later I inhale a whiff of Brylcream as Dad passes on his way to the fridge for a longneck. Something in the wool business, he owns a dozen shirts, all white, his ties all navy. Later, we clasp rosary beads and kneel before bedtime.

Another rack-turn in the toilet, fighting a grimace. Tears fill face-cracks between pleasure and pain.

Half dozen years of torment at the boys' secondary, run by the Brothers. And finally, I'm done. School's out forever. I buy albums of John Mayall's Bluesbreakers, Miles Davis, and New Order. I go to surf club dances. I drink from UDL cans and eat steaming chips. I buy my first car, a second-hand Ford Cortina, of duck-egg duco and wine-dark upholstery. I continue to attend Mass, where youth groups sing tunes from Godspell. I preferred it when they did Peter, Paul and Mary. I had a dog whose name was Blue. I had a little book was given to me and every page spelled liberty. All my trials…

Then the bank, and at last Ricky. He lends me a paperback with a blue cover: about war and madness, of laughter dark enough to sicken. It's some catch, that Catch-22. We lay waste to evenings, awash in Southern Comfort and Coke. It's never physical. Not that kind of love. A coupling of minds, fumbling soul closeness. Why have I never told my wife about him? I can't take Libby there. She smiles in straight lines. She wouldn't recognise his humour, a chortle from the gut. Deep laughter is not in her nature. And I can't admit to hearing cackles, as blackness swirls down to a sunless sea. In another hemisphere, even Ricky wouldn't recognise it.

With each crack and tear, the bowel movements shred more of me. By clenching my chin, I suppress additional outbursts.

A reunion of fifty-somethings, mostly Tory survivors of a Christian Brothers' education, synchronising life watches. Stomachs swell. Temples whiten. Scalps gleam. I'm not looking bad, on the outside. A few have checked out, not growing old as we grow old. Others show neon cheer. In place of sexual snickers, the old-young are full of wise saws and modern instances. Mate, they say. Maaaaaate. Soliloquies of feeling without admitting to any. I hear undertones they miss. I catch the hurt and confusion. Blokes who love their footy and cricket, who play tennis or golf. Some still jog. I feel marooned in their company, but I sense disinheritance, promises thwarted. One bloke mists up, admitting to mistreatment by the Christian Brothers. Can we talk about this? Can we emerge from shadow? No. We anaesthetise.

My best friend from those days is a dentist and a Liberal Party candidate. Kevin has money, yet he struggles, unable to understand his children or his ex-wife. Always a problem solver, he puts variables in a spreadsheet. Multiple tabs, he hastens to add, in case I think he's oversimplifying. Kevin has it logged to the nearest decimal point, putting his faith in a sigma function. I need to suppress laughter. His spreadsheet could stretch to infinity and never count angels on the head of a pin. But he must try.

Stretching membrane rips my toilet hell. Yet walls cannot contain me.

One day our suburban branch wakes to a university dropout. Rebel. Liberator. Artful dodger. Ricky latches onto me, the other member of his generation.

The first time Yossarian saw the Chaplain he fell madly in love with him.

We snigger for sanity. We drink. In the evenings we shriek to the *Young Ones* and watch porn. We experiment with weed, hash. We cackle so hard I can't tell where pain stops, and affection begins.

The mask freezes mid-smile. I clamp down on my howl, using breath control to sublimate spasms. Without Ricky I'd be no better than schoolmates trying to calibrate variables. He prised open my head to let in the light of hypocrisy, jingoism and lies by omission. He slashed with his Occam's razor, not just killing innocence but planting a bomb. With every page turn of a book it ticked louder, like an IRA bait to make ghosts of soldiers. When it went off, the blast shredded my soul, ripping out roots of God.

Finally, I'm strong enough to stand steady on the tiles. How long before I lack power to do this unaided? Ricky can't help. He left me in stages. Yet his university friends once again fill my kitchen. Denim darlings and blue-stocking babes who talk of schemes and glittering prizes. My windows face west to London or New York. I do not leave; the friends do. For a moment we sip champagne and puff joints. I share kisses with a girl who wears cornflowers and forget-me-nots in her hair. I hug blue-chip entrepreneurs, before they fly off to Oxford or Yale. Years gape a canyon. I cherish for no one's benefit.

And I resume with the Church, despite my doubts about entrusting our children to clergy, but Libby insists. They attend a parish school, suffering no more harm than other institutions. Secondary college, followed by university for each of them. Libby doesn't know the friends I once knew through Ricky, whose names I sometimes spy via the Facebook logo. She has never heard me mention Ricky. Long ago he vanished to finish his studies, then joined a corporation in the States. One time, I received a Christmas card signed 'Rick'. Someone from school, I told Libby. What do I fear from my wife?

Re-emerging in the corridor of a brother's beachfront home, I absorb his Aegean style vista. Feigning normality takes no effort. I've done it for years. Plenty of practice chatting with other Dads at sports days or scout nights, dying for decades. I stay put, while even the Church has moved on, paying off its paedophilia victims or discrediting them or relocating predators, just as the army disappeared Dunbar. My wife would not find it funny. Careless, I sometimes let irony seep through the cracks as I vibrate apart. She has caught me in Mass once or twice, grinning. It shears my gut, the laughter. Water leaks from my eyes.

Libby asks what's wrong.

~ Just a thing I read. It gave me the shivers. ~

~ From a book? ~

~ Uh…yes. About the Balkans. Centuries of brother killing brother. They call it 'ethnic cleansing,' like a pest control company. ~

~ You think that's funny? ~

~ Don't you? The sanitised language. The way they… Forget it. Not important. ~

People used to think me odd. Now they admire my strength. It's some catch, that Catch-22.

Despite how long I spend in the toilet, nobody comments.

~ Top-up? ~

I decline the beer. Easier to retreat into a corner and cast an eye over shelves of books arranged by colour. I would give them a personal nihil obstat but it's a poor selection. On my bus tomorrow I'll find solace with Seneca or Bede, or a solitary walker like Rousseau. At least they get the joke.

No one sees my collection: a Domesday Book of folly and waste chronicles, a menu for peace and war, for the quick and the dead. A silent categorical imperative, with consolations of Boethius and drolleries from Schopenhauer. Inconclusive evidence about an afterlife though. Dante offers no help, only reinforcing an Eden in the sky or a torment in Tartarus. I'm helped by apothegms from the Stoics as I assemble my codex for the end of all striving. A final train ride west, where bluebirds summon me with paradoxes between pages. Light meets dark amid the blank space, where secrets hide. Dying and alive at a junction, I can't share.

At home, I curl into an armchair, feet up. The movie puts Libby to sleep. I stretch for her hand but can't reach. Where are my wife's blueblood suitors now? Gone to dust, like her parents, like a thousand other shrivelled-up worries, mulching earth for worms.

Stars beckon through open curtains. I steal outside, then turn to look at our home: still part owned by the bank, with its garden of delphinium and morning glory. My wife glows cyan in TV light. When she wakes, Libby will find me out here, dwarfed by planets. We have a few moments yet. Venus, my morning and evening star, will supervise a great celestial drain. What do minutes matter?

Blowing air into my palms, I can still feel moisture. Coughing brings a speck of blood to my sleeve. Would it feel any better if I were struck by cholera or a British Airways crash at sea? Seneca knew two millennia ago, after learning from Zeno. Suns boil away. Moons crumble. New worlds thrive, only to turn extinct. Cosmic slapstick for the gods. Who's laughing now?

Yet I can't help it, giggling in falsetto. My feet climb stairs, past myriad identities stillborn. Is it a bridge to versions of me unrealised, in roles unplayed? I land in a place that cannot exist. Guests throb with empyrean gossip, clinking cocktails. Cambridge-scarved Guy Burgess dances with a woad-painted Boudicca, while Samuel Beckett bowls a leg-break to Stan McCabe, who hooks a catch to Nehru. Pythagoras applauds. Everyone's eyes brighten. No more gaps in understanding. To a trumpet chorus God arrives, resembling Alec Guinness. His mighty hand tosses a three-sided coin. Meanwhile the bearded maître d' must be St Peter, except he's the image of that homeless Krishna:

~ Good evening, sir. Smoking or non-smoking? ~

Rain speckles my face, or maybe it's Libby crying. Seated on flagstones with me, she cannot hear a snigger within. What did the great man write? 'If first you rid yourself of hope and fear, you have dismayed the tyrant's wrath.' I choose not to share consolations. My wife may brood on lawyers and finance, believing she knows the worst. I lack syntax to share. Past grief at not seeing our children reproduce, I wait. Empty-handed we arrive and go. The next class nears graduation but what will I miss? Climate degrading, debt rising. Libby should remarry; still handsome, despite crows' feet etching a fan at her eyes. I study moisture beads on those cheeks.

~ Feeling any better? ~

Time for more lies.

~ Just thinking about our wedding day. ~

Savouring a drum in her chest, I count its pulse. Aloud I recall an incident from one of our summers together.

Birds and traffic wake. Light from another sun will seek her out, ready to paint the sky.

11

Permission to Disappear

Edward Kus

I want to disappear
or to *splinter*
If I was a bird
I would fly south for the winter
How can the world
be so damn hard
and so devastatingly
beautiful
at the same time?

It is another autumn sunset
red and deep blue
the kind even the birds forget
to sing for, in awe of how *still*
this rushing world can be

My little son
is in hospital
fighting for his life
I cannot fly without him
so I must stay this season
Must stay, and now the birds are done
I sing a *minor* tune
to myself, or to the crooked trees
in shadows under the moon

Then, as if in answer
the drip machine is in song
calling the end of another infusion
a robotic, almost-currawong
we sing together in unison:

the sun has set but this one fights on

12

True Blue

Emma Jane Grey

'Fair dinkum bloke, that Bazza guy.
A true blue Aussie, through and through.'
True blues must work in 'real men' jobs.
They love a beer (or twenty-two).

'Hey, onya Bazza! Have one more!
Just chuck a sickie! She'll be right!'
True blue will always push his luck.
He'll show up drunk to building site.

'Report the guy! You showed up, right?
You did the bloody best you could!'
True blues' convictions can't be matched.
But Fair Work does just what they should.

'Hey take it easy, Bazza, mate!
I didn't force drinks down your gob!'
True blues don't make their own mistakes.
His friend's the one; lost him his job.

'I tell you what, mate, just sit down.
I'll show you how to make some cash.'
True blues don't hold their grudges long.
Not when they know they'll soon be trashed.

'Just take a punt, Baz. Pick your horse.
Or team, or man. Here, place your bets.'
True blues don't back down from a punt.
He knows he needs to clear his debts.

'No worries, mate! You'll win it back!
Not over 'til it's over, eh?'
True blues drink beer so they can't think.
And sporting bets don't go his way.

'Ah, cheer up, Baz! This round's on me!
And soon we'll do a Macca's run.'
True blues don't want to drink alone.
There's no such thing as 'nah, I'm done'.

'This place is (hic) a fucking hole.
Let's visit all my other haunts.'
True blues enjoy a good pub crawl.
Keep moving 'til they hear the taunts.

'Shit, here comes trouble. Mind my drink.
This loudmouth needs a lesson learned.'
True blues mark zones they think they own.
They truly think this space is earned.

'Hey you! That's right! The British dog!
What's that I heard you say to me?'
True blues will always escalate.
Pub crawl becomes pub brawling spree.

'Oh, bugger off ya limey prick.
Go back to where you came from, Stu.'
True blues accept no other voice.
Forget that they were migrants too.

13

Thirteen Uses for the Ties in Parliament House

after 'Thirteen Ways of Looking at the Old Tie' by John Agard

Lisa Collyer

A talking stick
of gender deafness.

A half-Windsor
for a blue-blood bind.

A direction
to a cubicle to cry into.

A prop for desk legs
to tie-up fresh meat.

A pacifier of reason
to dampen the shrill.

A traffic wand direction
to the prayer room.

A matrimonial knot
to keep her a *good wife.*

A silk gag
to muffle.

A tally-board
of intern conquests.

A vertical entry
into a token MP.

In Hansard's record
the tie could inexplicably be:

the nose behind
the stiff in the pew,

big swinging dicks
unlike the real thing.

14

a brief flirtation with ~~you~~ blue

Paris Rosemont

Let's get the rhinoceros out of the way: I have an ugly birthmark. On my goddam left cheek, the size of a ten-cent piece. Hey, eyes up—my face is up here, buddy. It's fucking blue. (The fugly birthmark, that is.) A *Mongolian spot,* they call it. How quaint. I'M NOT EVEN A FUCKIN' MONGOL. But I guess that would be of little concern to dear Erwin Otto Eduard von Bälz, were he alive to note the culturally insensitive term he coined in the 1800s is still in circulation today and treading on the tiny golden lotus feet of neo-geishas. *What? I'm conflating cultures? Don't sweat it, mate. Same same, but different. Appropriation's a dirty word. We're all true-blue ocker here. Born and bred [from imported parts]. It'll all (b)leach out in the (white)wash.* I mean, everyone still calls 'Red Ripperz' *Red Skins* and 'Scalliwags' *Golliwogs...*

you can rebrand shit
but crap by any other
name will still stink foul

I call bullshit on blue balls, by the way. Whether white-collar workers or blue-collar boys, they all squirm the same as they complain *we* turn them on too much. It's practically our *duty* to relieve them. And so, we get on our knees and do what *good girls* do. Golly gee, those balls are no longer blue.

Was Little Boy Blue
blowing more
than his horn?
The cornfields are all ears...

I didn't have *something blue* on my wedding day. I'm partial to snapdragons and hollyhocks, but my bouquet hadn't a whisker of cornflower. The Ezy-Mart next to the Registry proffered only carnations or day-old roses in ultramarine tubs near the checkout (marked down by $2, as they had already started to brown at the edges). Take a ticket for birth or death certificates. Marriages upstairs. It was like going through the public hospital system. We were issued the next celebrant off the rank. It was unfussy and unsentimental. I thought I didn't have anything blue with me on my wedding day, but I'd been wrong. It turns out I'd been colour-blind—*I'd* been blue all along.

Q. What does blue taste like?
A. Slushies and brain freeze, the nose
of Bubble O' Bill.

Kindergarten armed me with a starter box of 16 Crayolas. As my appreciation for nuance deepened, I expanded to sets of 24–48–64 and beyond. I learned to pirouette from *Periwinkle* to *Robin's Egg* through to the perfume of *Prussian Blue.* Nineteen *Bluetiful* variations on a theme. I long to scrawl on a *Midnight Blue* sky: *To Sir, With Love.* Though my *Sir* was a *Miss.* Many *Misses.* I miss them. *(There's Oedipal baggage to unpack in that.)*

Oh, *Nina, Nina, pretty ballerina* will you also indulge me by singing the blues? I want to inhale the Chet Baker hues, your bluest of *Blue Thoughts.* Give me *Blue Velvet* more than once in a *Blue Moon.* There's a strange comfort in mopping the floor with one's tears. (Just don't go *Betty Blue* on me, *s'il vous plaît et merci!*)

Let me swoon over your *Blue Suede Shoes,* you handsome devil, you. Daydream of someday finding myself in that *Blue Bayou,* with Jimmy waiting on a fishing boat in *Blue Jeans* and a white shirt with his fresh catch of blue fin tuna and even fresher twinkle in his baby blues, ready to sail off with me into *that familiar sunrise* over the *Pacific Blue* as *happy little bluebirds fly beyond the rainbow.* Mister Dean's a right gentleman who wouldn't be so crass as to ask a lady whether she had a bruise on her cheek.

My motherfuckin' face is not an exotic 'oriental' curiosity abounding *in nature's gifts of beauty rich and rare* for you to comment upon, even though you do. You corner me into an admission that's none of your bloody business. *Yes—it's a bruise. I…uh, fell down the stairs…* Or *No—it's just a fuckin' ugly birth defect.* Either will leave you wishing you hadn't asked. I hold my breath and bite my tongue. Your probing questions leave me red, blanched, and blue in the face.

15

Shades of Hostility

Afifa Kamal Chaudhry

Today, my gynaecologist told me that I have a hostile uterus. She explained something about the uterus lining on the diagram laminated under her glass desk. The diagram of this hostile organ was in different shades of blue. Ovaries in cobalt blue, spongy bits around the tube in periwinkle blue, and vagina in sky blue. I asked her if my uterus was blue. She said no.

On the way back I stopped at the Magic Corn stall on Mall Road. The young boy preparing my masala corn was wearing an odd shade of blue, turquoise when he moved out of the shade to grab the chili sauce, and Tiffany Blue when he leaned back to look for a paper cup under the little cart. I briefly thought about telling him that I only have a sixteen percent chance of getting pregnant, but I decided against it. I kept watching him and wondered about the other eighty-four percent. The corn tasted disgusting.

At night I told Haroon, my husband, about the sixteen percent. He looked very hurt and for three complete minutes said nothing, only stood under the doorway. I had to look away because I knew I would start laughing. He then hugged me. I thought about expressing some kind of pain, a look, or a little cry. I knew he wanted me to, so I let him hug me and rub my back and whisper things into my ear.

*

When I was eight, my mother took me to the railway station in Ranipur after she fought with my father. This was the first time I ever saw the outside of the haveli. We walked to the outskirts through the tiny bazaar, uneven roads, and barren plains. From the bazaar, she brought me pink threads clustered in a plastic bag. I had never had cotton candy before. It tasted sweet and papery and I liked it. I wanted to buy some for Haider, my elder brother, but my mother said no. I wanted to ask her why she didn't bring any of my brothers along, but I was too scared.

Instead at the station when she asked me to sit quietly beside her on a bench I complied. She wasn't waiting for a train; I knew this because so many had passed, yet she didn't move once. There were many people around us; men in wrinkled white shalwar passing by would stare at my mother, and women in dark chaddars whispered around. Some people were getting off trains and some were waiting for them. My mother and I were just sitting. We kept sitting on that bench until our shadows enlarged. She turned towards me.

What would happen if I jumped in front of one of these trains?

She folded her hands in her lap and asked me. Her braid was still intact, not a hair out of place but her ears were missing the gold hoops she liked wearing. Her shalwar kameez was creased and her dupatta which would be draped around her head from the moment she woke up in the haveli was hanging around her neck.

The train would stop. I said and looked down. I really didn't know what would happen.

Look up. Look at me. She hissed. *Nothing would happen. People die and nothing happens.*

Her hands around my bare arms tightened.

Every day I wake up and think about killing your father. Do you know why I haven't yet?

I shook my head.

Because of the four months and ten days of confinement, I will have to endure. That's all. He is just not worth all the planning and the religious custom. I don't want to mourn him.

She let go of me and turned back to watching the train leave. Some hours later my father came and took us back to the haveli.

*

My days at Kinnaird College changed me. I left the haveli in Ranipur and moved to a hostel in Lahore. I chose Psychology as my major because it seemed like a subject that I could understand comfortably but not excel in. My skin stopped smelling of ghee; instead I started using a lavender night cream that Paras, my roommate, had recommended. I stopped praying because my mother wasn't there to tell me to. I stopped wearing monochrome shalwar kameez and wore sarees as Paras did. I was out of the four walls of the red haveli, yet I felt more confined than ever.

In the summer of 1998, Paras took me to Karachi where I met Haroon at a dinner party. It is true that I took an instant liking towards him, but it wasn't love or lust. He had just completed law school in Warwick and was back in Pakistan to take over his father's law firm. He was energetic enough to make me listen to what he was saying and was shallow enough to stop me from arguing with him about his beliefs. There were many people around him but when he talked, he only looked at me and I liked that. For the first time, I was able to hold a man's attention. I felt powerful.

The day after that dinner party, Haroon came to the apartment I was staying in. He talked and I listened but this time there was no one else to compete for his attention. It was just me and him. I didn't like that. I have only liked Haroon when there are other people around to witness his commitment towards me but when we are alone in the vicinity of our bedroom, I feel trapped and silly. Haroon knows this too because a day before I was meant to leave Karachi, he invited me to have dinner with his family, where proposed to me in front of them. I said yes.

*

The warden had sent a girl to our room to tell us that there was a call for me. I was laying upside-down on my bed. Paras was on the floor with fashion magazines spread out in front of her. She was looking for pictures of Sanjay Dutt to cut out and stick to the wall which was already filled with pictures of actresses with big hair and anorexic models.

It makes throwing up easier after eating, Paras explained. *When I look at these actresses and models, I want to be like them and when I look at Sanjay, I want to be with him but that can only happen if I am skinny.*

I contemplated whether to go down or take a nap. While descending the stairs I wondered who would call me. I talked to Haroon yesterday and specifically asked him to call me next week rather than every day. On the last step, I realised I wasn't wearing any shoes. My feet were wet. For a moment

I thought about running up to my room to get my slippers. The warden at the desk handed me the receiver.

Hello.

Are you coming home for the summer holidays? It was my mother.

Probably not. I am staying with Paras.

Is she your mother now?

Are you?

She didn't say anything. If she hadn't been breathing so heavily, I would have thought that she had hung up. It was April. Sun had just set. Lahore looks different when the sunsets. It looks crueller.

Ghar ajao. [*Come home.*] That was the last time I talked to her.

*

Sometimes I worry I know too much and sometimes I worry I know too little. When I am with older married women who think I am too modern and young hormonal boys who think I am too easy, I feel far superior. I talk about politics, history, literature, and music. I use words I know they won't know the meaning of, I quote lines from books I know they haven't read and probably never will. I talk about changing the world only because I know they don't want to. It makes me feel better about myself. I feel like a radical. The line between my class and all the others blurs and I can be anyone I want to be, a radical.

When I am alone with a book, reading words I can't comprehend and ideas that don't diffuse into my brain, I feel like a fraud. I think I have just memorised some words and use only them in conversation and writing. I think I have just memorised dates and years, but I don't know what actually happened. I think I have memorised names of people I don't think ever existed, but I quote them in conversation a lot. I am a fraud. An imposter who spent years in a grammar school and tried to befriend the elite, went to a private liberal arts college, wore chiffon sarees, drank, and smoked to only fit in. I don't read anymore. Books confront me and I don't want that. I don't want to feel inferior. I gave up my mother to sound smart at dinner parties, yet I feel dumb.

Sometimes in bed, I pretend that I love Haroon. I act kind. I hide how repulsed I feel when he is near me. Sometimes I wish Haroon was my brother.

The idea of sharing a womb with him is more exciting than the practice of sharing a bed with him. I could have easily loved him as a sister.

*

A month after we got married, Haroon said that I should see a psychiatrist. We were in Scotland for our honeymoon. It was raining outside.

Do you think I am sick in the head?

That is not what I said.

Now that you have fucked me you think there is something fundamentally wrong with me.

I didn't mean that and you know it.

Was I not good in bed?

Please stop.

The rain outside reminded me of Lahore in October. Lahore in October is different, it's more foreign. Haroon was sitting on an armchair five feet away from the bed where I was sitting. On the side table next to the bed was an empty bottle of cheap red wine which we both had drunk last night. I grabbed it and threw it across the room. It shattered on the cream-coloured wall behind Haroon.

You bitch.

He left the room and came back two hours later. We both apologised to each other.

*

I didn't go to my mother's funeral, nor did I cry. I wanted to go and mourn her, but I didn't know where to go and which existence of hers to mourn. I didn't know how to separate life from her or ghee from her skin or pink from her shalwar kameez or cold from her bones or disappointment from her tongue. They buried her under a tree in the red haveli because my father thought it was what she had always wanted. No one exactly knows how she died. They all woke up one day and she was dead in her room. I still wonder how they realised she was dead. If it were me, I would have never known.

*

My mother gave birth to four children, three sons, and one daughter. When pregnant with the fifth, she threw herself down the stairs after a fight with my father and miscarried. They wrapped the little ball of flesh and bone in a white cloth and buried it in the family graveyard five miles outside the haveli. My father cried a lot, the midwife had told him it was a boy. I can never forget the content on my mother's face when she saw my father crying, the most satisfied my father and I had ever seen her. She was strangely happy.

Haider, my eldest brother, was the only brother I loved. During his time in college, he joined a militant group that believed in liberating Kashmir, from what I don't know. The group supplied weapons to the Mujahideen, mostly just kitchen knives as they didn't have enough funding to buy guns and didn't know where to buy them from. Haider was oddly close to my mother, our mother, to the point I once even accused them of incest, which they both never denied. I was jealous. Jealous knowing that my mother was capable of loving any child of hers. Two days after our mother died Haider killed himself. The militant group didn't tell us for months, fearful that his suicide would damage the group's work. He had cut his wrists with one of the kitchen knives they were planning to snuggle into Kashmir. They were now one knife and one man short. They wouldn't tell us where they buried him, and I am glad they didn't.

Then there is Zaki, the son my mother gave birth to and forgot. Zaki was a quiet child. No one really cared if he was there or not. Nobody questioned his absence nor his existence. I think he felt that too, so after high school, he moved abroad. I don't know where he is now but once or twice a year I get postcards from him, sometimes from Italy and sometimes from Germany. Zahir, my father's favourite, lives in Islamabad with his young wife and two ugly children. They visit me sometimes. His young wife always gives me the telephone number of good fertility doctors in Lahore. Zahir was an ideal child or my father's ideal child. Often, I would see my father and him strolling in the garden with my father's arm around Zahir's shoulders. He is my father's successor. The haveli belongs to him, his young wife, and two ugly children. Sometimes, I wish he was dead instead of Haider.

*

There is a Sufi shrine in Lahore where all women with a hostile uterus go. My mother-in-law explained that one of our distant relatives who had been married for fifteen years with no child visited the shrine every day for three months. A year later, she had twins and a year after that she had another child. It sounded very promising. Haroon wanted to go with me, but I said no. Lahore is very unwelcoming in December. I took off my shoes in the car and walked towards the blue domes.

16

bruised

Pat Saunders

it's blue today
yesterday it was crimson red
tomorrow it will be green
the day after
yellow

blue is when it's most tender
to touch
blue means steering clear of trouble
doing everything right
avoiding a misstep; 'a blue'
to ensure
there's no reason for it to be touched
eggshells everywhere
hoping with all my heart there's no crack

blue isn't too bad to look at
this blue's camouflaged by my Garfield tattoo
barely visible
blooming beneath his belly
unseen by accidental eyes

17

Quick Exit

after Marcel Duchamp's
Nude Descending a Staircase, No. 2
(1912)

Maria Bonar

Naked, wearing only bruises
she flees down the staircase
dripping a spotted blood trail
on the wooden slats.

Yesterday's iris-bloom injuries
purple and yellow, overlaid by
today's cyanotic blue. A necklace
of thumbprints. Face unmarked.

Her husband/tormenter/Janus
keeper of the key and doorways
snores sour alcoholic breaths
in the debris of their bedroom.

In this house, his true visage
revealed. Cruel, condescending
brutal, unlike the urbane cultured
face he presents to the world.

This time, the need for survival
outweighs her terror.
In the hallway, snatches a
raincoat, purse, his keys.

Takes money from his wallet.
Feet pushed into her gardening
clogs. Spreads her wings
takes flight into a new day.

18

Vessel

Elena Disilvestro

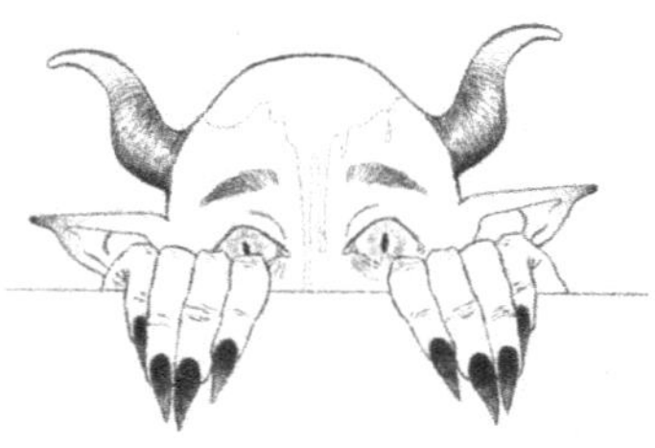

Few would deny a woman's purpose is to be possessed.

From the very first moment the spectre enters her stomach, she appears rosier. And when it erupts out of her ribcage, she knows her life is fulfilled. What could a woman hope to accomplish beyond her role as a vessel?

Few would contend this—and even fewer as vehemently as me. And yet here I stand, barefoot in the woods, calling out to spirits. The whole thing is ridiculous of course, but I'm here all the same. Through the gnarled trunks and branches, I see others. They're nestled further into the forest, fog diffusing their silhouettes. Very few, like me, call out dispiritedly, likely forced to attend this ordeal by someone else in their frustrated lives. Around them, the most traditional of all cast snooty glances and curl their lips; to those ladies this is no small matter—it is our innate duty! But there are others too: adorned with smiles so wide their cheeks must hurt. Those ladies sing melodies to attract the spectres, joyously waiting for the moment they've dreamt of for so many years. How desperately I wish I could be one of them.

But I'm simply not. No matter what others say to me, no matter how many times I try to be lenient and consider a future as a vessel, I feel no desire for that to come to pass. But if I am to be here, I might as well make my attempt convincing.

I cup my hands around my mouth and call out once more. Dirt cakes under my toenails as I walk, the hem of my dress tracking mud behind me. The river is but a short walk away and the ground is still slick with the residue of its flooded waters. I continue this way for several minutes, but I keep out of the thickets, lest someone actually answers. The trees loom above me as I go. They are nearly colourless under the moonlight and the wind whistles as it moves through their leafless branches.

Just as I am sure that no spirits will come to us tonight, I hear a delighted squeal. I turn sharply and there, just a few meters to my left, stands a woman shaking in anticipation. Before her a small sphere of cerulean light floats, thin tendrils unfurling from it and extending towards her. The wisps curl as they near her—like knobbly fingers with too many joints. She spreads her arms in welcome and gently closes her eyes. Instantly, the wisps seize her.

Her neck, her arms, her legs. Tendrils greedily envelop every inch of skin they find. But most of all they grab onto her lower stomach. As they wrap around her, they grow, from the thinness of spun sugar to thick coils of rope. I want to scream, to run and rip the fingers off her body. But I stand, rooted to the ground, eyes glued to her expression. Her smile comes easy, the tears in the corners of her eyes born from joy. She wants this, I tell myself, she was born for this moment. I don't believe it, of course, but that doesn't matter much.

The coils tighten so much I worry they'll squeeze her out of her skin like mince from a casing until the end of a wisp—one of the few that remain cobweb-thin—finds purchase in her stomach. A little hole, put there by a knife before she stepped into the woods, matching the cut on my stomach—the cut on the stomach of all women who come into the woods. There, the wisp slithers into her body like a serpent and soon the rest of the spirit follows. All the tendrils unfurl and race into her insides, squeezing through the tiny gap until there's nothing left.

The woman collapses onto her knees, exhausted and elated. Soon, everyone rushes to her, to lift her up again and congratulate her. To carry her back to the village and await the big day.

*

'THE RIVER! THE WATERS!'

Bells ring throughout the village, drowned only by the stomping of feet. Months have passed since we ventured into the forest and the river has finally flooded. The waters have broken the barriers, and that can only mean one thing.

The big day is upon us.

I run through the commotion, headed straight to the sanctum—already late despite my haste. Ahead, I can see them carrying her into the dim room, candles casting uncanny shadows across her face. I catch up to them just as the great stone doors begin to close. I slip inside and cover my ears as the doors slam forcefully shut.

Lowering my hands, I blink rapidly to adjust my gaze. She is wriggling with discomfort, her stomach expanded to an unimaginable degree. And yet she is not angry. She is not even frustrated. No, behind her pain and struggle, she feels what can only be described as glee. Again, I wonder why I cannot be like her, why I cannot consider this the blessing she deems it to be.

But there's no more time for pondering because the waters have started pouring through the cracks and the floor is growing wetter by the second. The preacher arrives promptly, book in his sharp-nailed hand, and we all get to work. Some hold her hands, others her feet. I stand back at the ready with a pint of fresh milk. The preacher opens the book, clears his throat twice, and then the exorcism begins.

As soon as the words fall from his lips, I see her arch her back and scream in pain. Her limbs thrash, but the others hold her down. They've done this before. Unfazed, the preacher continues, the language ancient, his words brusque. She flails and flails, head wildly whipping from side to side. Her eyes are wild and unfocused, the scream that was once human now resembling that of tortured hounds. She wants this, I tell myself, she was born for it.

Another ancient sentence and she begins floating, her body lifting off the ground as though suspended by her midsection. Here she is released from the others' grip, finally free to thrash as wildly as she pleases. Two more ancient sentences and suddenly she stiffens. Her limbs jerk once, then twice, then fall limply at her sides. Slowly, the mass in her stomach migrates upwards until it sits behind her ribs. Silence engulfs the air as the preacher awaits the beginning of the next stage. Silence.

Silence.

Then a clear snap, like breaking twigs.

She is screaming again. She wants this, I tell myself, she was born for it. The preacher continues his sermon, and the twigs of her ribs continue to break. And then a ghostly hand breaks free from her insides, a spray of warm blood fizzing out of the middle of her sternum where it escaped. It catches me in the face, and it takes all I have to not bend over and hurl the contents of my stomach all over the sanctum's floor. By the time I look back at her, her mouth is frothing, and the ghost is crawling out of her ribcage.

It is a translucent periwinkle—semi-corporeal and the size of a house cat. It has two sharp-nailed hands with which it crawls its way out and a glowing stare that flits disoriented across the room. That's not right, I think, I don't care what she was born for.

'What are you waiting for, woman?! The milk!'

Damn it! I curse myself under my breath for getting distracted. One quick shake to refocus and I am hurling the pint of milk onto the poltergeist. It splashes all over it, washing some blood off the woman. The ghost detaches fully from its vessel and gurgles with glee, diving towards the ground to lick the spilt milk. Gently, the woman's body lowers to the ground. As her eyes blink awake, she finds my gaze.

'Congratulations,' I say so meekly not even I am convinced.

She is breathing heavily and utterly weak, sprawled on the ground while the others tend to her wounds. She seems to confuse my horror with jealousy, for she turns to me and says: 'Don't worry, you'll get chosen soon enough.' Then she smiles, a smile no one in her state has any right to smile. I smile too and hope I don't appear as harrowed as I feel.

After she is carried away and the poltergeist escorted out with her after the blood is washed off the sanctum floor and my face, I sit at the edge of the river under a pallid moon. The others are getting ready, nicking their stomachs and discarding their shoes. The search for spectres is always more bountiful after the river has flooded.

As they begin to file out towards the woods I follow. But as they slow down and spread out, I continue onwards. Some notice and call after me, but my feet don't slow. I walk until my calves ache until the lights of the village are as distant as the stars above me. Until dawn breaks and rich veins of orange and red fill the sky.

The trees thin out as I reach the end of the woods, replaced by blades of grass that glitter with dew. I look up and let the light wash over me, warmth seeping through. The sky is clear and unbroken by clouds, a vibrant blue so different from the pallid, purplish one I've grown used to. My steps don't slow, but my gaze is transfixed.

Unchosen, I venture forth. The harvest in the bag over my shoulder is plentiful; my shoes are sturdy, my stomach uncut.

19

Rayleigh Scattering

Taylor Johnson

Fifty thousand vessels bobbing in a bathtub. Plastic toys pitching and rolling with moronic grins painted over their bows. Criss-crossing a primordial sea that existed long before anything else.

Fifteen thousand microscopic containers stacked onboard each vessel. Seven hundred and fifty million containers total, one bathtub. Every single item, every manufactured unit, every possible noun, packaged and organised, bobbing in a bathtub.

Forty figurines per vessel. Each figurine: one yellow sou'wester, one oilskin jacket. Two million figurines total, one bathtub. They move, stop-motion, in-between the containers. Occasionally catching panoramas of a colossal ceramic wall.

The best job I ever had was on one of these toy ships. Rotate twenty-five days at sea, three days on land. At port we'd assemble skyscrapers out of shipping containers, each time fashioning a new economic metropolis. *Venice on Wheels* was our name for it. At the next port we'd level it to nothing, no trace would remain, that was the rule.

The best days were at sea. Nothing to do but check monitors and piss in the breeze. If the sky was wide and the sea was flat Captain Burke would let us play football on the foredeck in-between the towers. I could only play for a short while before my heartbeat would syncopate. The company doctors had diagnosed heart arrhythmia on my first voyage following a black out on the gangway. All I remembered was being face first on the welded metal, bleary vision through gaps. The sou'wester toppling off my head and swinging into the choppy surf.

At times the arrhythmia felt like someone else's pulse moving through me. Someone a few steps into the future who knew trouble was brewing before I did. Another person's heart going all a-flutter. It happened when

Captain Burke called me onto bridge one year into my service. Hand on the carved doorknob—a three-beat waltz in my chest.

Well meaning, but a completely useless twat—was our little epigram for Captain Burke. Spindly-limbed and in obvious, desperate, need of a pharmaceutical solution for chronic nerves, he sat rattling in the Captain's chair. A mighty seafarer's beard, that was his description of the sparse patches of fur around his lip. He got up and down about three times before uttering anything of value. Stepping away from the desk he'd rest against a shelf which was just a little too high for his shoulder, offer some polite question on how I was settling in, or the weather, or otherwise inane, then return to his seat. Eventually he gave up the chase.

'There's a new, ah, Captain comin' aboard...well they're coming aboard and I'm going *off-board*...I guess you could say. A Mr Westlake will be taking my position is what I'm trying to say', I winced at the weak smile the man was willing into existence, 'I'm telling everyone one by one, because, you see, *they feel*...the *company feels*... I might have been a bit soft on you lot, and they've brought this one on board to help. Apparently, a bit of a hard nose, but out to impress is my, ah...gathering...*suspicion...guess!*'

Why did I feel so devastated for Burke? I couldn't recall a single warm moment together. Apparently during the blackout he'd stood by, mute, tapping fingertips urgently against his own pant leg. Yet I couldn't picture what could be waiting for him back on land. All I saw was Burke holed up, hours on end, eyes through a window carved out of the ceramic, fixed on the big blue.

Captain Westlake appeared at the next port-of-call. There were no witnesses to his coming aboard but by the next crew meeting he was there, standing atop a table in the messroom. His face must have hung two metres over everyone else. It dawned on us that this must be an intentional move, noting the formal instruction that *all* crew *must* remain seated *throughout* the meeting. I sat next to old Rayleigh, and we made a game of spotting ourselves in the new Captain's aviator sunglasses. Rayleigh was an odd one. Been crewed on the same ship for all of forty years but never scrubbed a deck or loaded a single container. He was the sole employee of the Research Wing on the second deck. The story was that, out of debt and desperation, the company had cut the size of crew rooms in half to make rental space which they advertised to universities and scientists; maritime real estate being incredibly lucrative while the ceramic cliffs were overcrowded and the floating shanty towns too dangerous. Many scientific ventures failed in the harsh conditions, but Rayleigh's particular research thrived.

Lithely and bewhiskered, Rayleigh looked a better sailor than anyone else onboard. Special accommodations were afforded so that he kept a white sou'wester and oilskin, a nice match to the chalky curtain hanging off the base of his balding head. He also smoked a pipe, something none of us had ever seen before.

Whenever the weather was wild and I had a little free time, I'd lounge in a corner of Rayleigh's office, tinkering with dismantled instruments left on the bench. Rayleigh usually forgot I was there, gasses and light being his only muse. Puffs of argon, xenon or radon perpetually circuited the office through a looping, spiralling network of tubes. From floor to ceiling glass invaded all available space in an ordered chaos that only he understood. If he was seated behind the desk all you could spot of Rayleigh was his bald dome, lolling at the centre of all these deranged orbits.

After Westlake's inaugural speech we sat in Rayleigh's office. A panelled window behind the desk framed the port as it receded out of view into an afternoon abyss. Turquoise water gifted its reflection, filtering through the transparent instruments and dancing over the walls. It was quieter than usual between us. I commented that, who knows, maybe the crew will take to Westlake's glasses, and we'd soon be inundated with a flock of aviator seamen, sneering mindlessly across the deck; Rayleigh didn't stir. A common adage was that Rayleigh was impossible to read. Inside, you pictured a whirling mass of scientific pondering, a swelling thunderhead of turbulent, contradicting propositions. But the end goal of all this research was a mystery. Clearly the company took great interest in it, having continued an unfavourable leasing arrangement for four decades without word or hassle. But Rayleigh said very little on what this was all leading too, just that it was 'global' and that the best working days were clear and windless.

Something seemed to deeply unsettle Rayleigh about Westlake. Every few minutes he would swivel to the window and cast a glance over the ship's patterned wake.

At one point he stretched his neck skywards. 'One hundred and fifty million miles to the sun'.

His back turned to me, the voice ricocheted off the window and diffracted through the room. 'For most of the way it's blackness, nothingness—shut your eyes, it's the same effect…', he spoke as if he'd personally been there. 'But at the beginning there's six thousand miles of atmosphere; we can breathe, there's light, there's blue.'

The next day I woke to a rumba rhythm beating in my chest. I went down to breakfast in the dining area but couldn't find Rayleigh. After eating I tried his office and the adjacent laboratory, both doors locked—I couldn't remember ever seeing that before. I knocked to no reply. Lunch, dinner, also absent.

The siren sounded around twelve o'clock the following day as I was running safety checks on top deck, and from there the entire crew began a top-to-bottom search.

Two days later Westlake led me into Rayleigh's office. The widest shoulders you've ever seen blocked out the window and trailed an ugly shadow that shrank the room. From the moment he skirted open the little curtain cloistering my bunk, unannounced and unwelcome, and throughout our merry journey across the ship, it was clear the Captain's suspected I was involved, somehow, in the disappearance. Unsubtle probes were fired into every past interaction and every known affiliation. I didn't have much to say. A few times I thought I caught the Captain standing a little taller in the passageways, raising himself on tip-toes. I had to bite my tongue.

Wrapping his knuckles over a beaker suspended in Rayleigh's office, like a dirty child disturbing a fish tank, Westlake changed tack onto Rayleigh's research. He questioned what exactly the old man was doing down here anyway. There was a tone suggesting Westlake already knew the answer. I replied that I didn't know like *technically* what he was doing, but you got, you know, a sense of it.

'And what sense was that?', the Captain's hands pilfering random papers out of the desk draw.

'Ah, a bunch of things, light waves, lasers, aerodynamics, refraction *whatever that is*, God.'

'Did you say God?' Eyes tightening on me. 'What's *God* got to do with it?' I squeezed around the bulky Minotaur of a man to the window. With a quiver I clicked open the latch and slid the pane upwards to reveal a tossing, nauseous surf forgotten under our feet. I stretched a finger out into the briny air and jabbed it skywards.

'Anything to do with up there, he wanted to know about it.'

Things did not improve after that. I was stood down from all duties indefinitely and informed that a contract re-evaluation was expected at the next port. The mere suggestion of port sent cold nerve pain up my neck. The feeling of land crept in, of sweaty human compaction dominating every faculty. Endless walking through hollowed out corridors that curved too low overhead. I didn't know how I could survive if I went back. There was always chatter of new initiatives to make use of the surface world. Promises of open plains and monstrously high vistas over the water. Some said scientists were close to debonding the components of grout and creating soils that could support plant life. Leaflets would pass hand-to-hand illustrating high-tech communities thriving under unobstructed sunlight. Villages of domed buildings, each home sporting a white letterbox and picket-fence. Homes neighbouring fungi pastures or ponds teeming with multicoloured dots that represented the new edible micro-organisms that had been discovered. Nothing ever came of it all though, and meanwhile people kept digging deeper into the ceramic and catching fish in greater and greater numbers.

Days went by, inert, absorbed in the scratches on the underside of the top bunk. A beatnik jazz band swinging under my ribcage. A fellow seaman whispered through the curtain, 'Something's going on with one of the containers…everyone thinks err…you need to take a look'. Suddenly the band started accenting the off beats.

Sea water ran in constant motion over the foredeck. As I made my way along I lost sight of my feet in the turbulent froth. A clump of sailors stood around the base of a container stack, each either covering their breath or turned away to face the oncoming surf. Some saw me coming and pointed towards the stack. 'It REEKS.'

It was as if some colossal goddess had slipped on the firmament. A vial had spilled from her palm, its contents falling to earth and dousing the deck. A strange, viscous concoction she'd usually kept locked in her nightstand draw. The tower of containers was streaked in a strange chalky lilac. If you lent in closely, strong fumes would rip up the nasal passage and shoot sparks over your frontal lobes. In the sun this thick substance had set into a bubblegum tac with ridged peaks.

One of the sailors handed me a sou'wester, a thin spray of lilac dust flinging from the plastic as it moved. It had been hanging off the side of the container, they told me. Inside there was a label: RAYLEIGH.

I stretched out my palm, eager to feel the alien surface. As I drew closer in, the fumes began to sear on the intake of breath. I was millimetres from the surface when a voice jolted out of the clear blue.

'Releasing that scumbag scientist I see.' Westlake was sailing like an airborne starfish from the second container up. One hand hooked through a gap in the steel and one foot lodged underneath, the remaining limbs waved freely as the deck tossed from side to side.

'You know and I know', Westlake boomed into the sky, 'that Mr Rayleigh has scurried away into this here container. Locked himself inside rather than give up his secrets.'

The sea wind whistled through a gap in Westlake's words. 'Secrets, I'll remind, that are really the world's to know. It may be of interest to you all to learn that Mr Rayleigh has done something marvellous. See, when a snotty child next asks his poor mother, "oh momma do you know why the sky so blue?" She can answer, "Of course, Mr Rayleigh taught us"'.

A strange reaction spread over the group. At first there was a little snickering on account of Westlake's enlivened performance, which he had committed to with a cutesy high-pitched voice. But once the meaning of the words rose above the scene, it dawn on them what Rayleigh had been up to all these years, and the snickering slid into a kind of bemusement.

For me meanwhile, John Bonham had crawled inside my chest cavity. He was playing the gig of his life, showing the world his triplet bass kick. 'Now its very important that we pull old Rayleigh out from here. You open up that door and pull him out.'

A remote voice took hold of me. There was no way out for me from here, I could see that I'd end up on land no matter which way I chose to go. My palm thrust out, jabbing into the side of the container. There was a puff of purple as the steel shell cracked like tempered chocolate. Westlake wobbled as the container he was clinging to began to fold into itself. The entire structure crumbled in an instant, the first domino in the chain. It only took one violent sway to affect all the other towers loaded on the ship. Then, one by one they slid overboard, the collapse bringing on an overpowering sound, the thumping and pounding of steel freight against the ocean. Under the force of movement some containers burst at the seams, spewing packaged goods into the blue.

It was surprising how quickly the cargo spread; at first there was a circular blob surrounding the ship, a lifeless amoeba. Then, spreading further, it took the form of Rayleigh. A scientist, on his back, adrift in the bathtub. Eyes pointed upwards into the blue he'd once found. The man who discovered blue, floating in a stream of red.

20

Blues for John

Richard Calam

1 River

When I was a child, this river spoke as a child.
All the arms of ghost gums were like
boys' arms, clean and free. The mud banks,
slippery like wet leather, smelled of freshness
not decay. Lost bicycles and abandoned prams
bore no signs of public loss or private tragedy.

As always, junk meant nothing. The water gushed
round it like bells of hand-blown glass.
Every prospect of impending doom sank
among green reeds susurrating peacefully.

But now I am a man and you are gone,
this river sees me as a man. All its eddies are
my eddies. All its pools of standing moonlight
mirror in my mind the Prussian blue haunting
nocturnes of middle-age remorselessly.

On these nights at riverside, each cold star
finds its place on the still face of black ponds
and every shadow I'm afraid of steals across
the hollows and the hopes I hide in breathlessly.

This much was spared you, John:
seeing the river still like a child when
you have to take it all so seriously.

When I was a child, this river spoke as a child.
Together we saw the twist of it before us.
In our minds we walked the runnels to the delta,
but on your own you went further into daylight
past tide of time and matter where all rivers
glint and shimmer before bleeding out to sea.

2 *Sea*

Remember: the vacant coast,
the banks of beached sea kelp,
the prints in sand, and the ruts
and rivulets that wove in streaks
down to undomesticated sea.

Remember: the smell of rot,
fresh sea salt, and the
red cliffs' outlaw cactus—
belligerent, tall and old.

Remember: thistle blown
like microscopic cells across
the arc of summer's azure sky.

Remember: the screes of shale,
the sun-warmed rock and,
behind that, Norfolk pines with
programs of growth that dwarfed
everything so comprehensively.

Remember: the indifferent clouds,
the formless sand, the
indeterminate sun that
touched your shoulders as I saw
women touch them absently.

Remember: how we walked the
landscape of young men
listening to the wind or
searching under rocks for
signs of God or absent fathers,
knowing no one ever really knows
what it means to witness
works of truth, works of deity.

And I remember that it always
made you smile to think there
was never any rationale for you
any more than there would ever
be convincing rationale for me.

Remember: the vacant coast,
the banks of beached sea kelp,
the prints in sand.

21

Wetland Walk

Sharon Kernot

The water is flanked by eucalypts, wattle, reeds, and rushes.
There are swamp hens, moor hens, black ducks, and grebes.
No blue-billed ducks today, but the bushes
are blue in parts with the iridescence of fairy wrens
that skip and hop across the path
you walk, noting the latest fallen trees—
the way they seem to rest overnight
sometimes in the water, sometimes leaning against another.
The pobblebonks serenade you as you weave
your way over and around the many lakes
hoping, always, to catch sight or sound
of something different. Today the sky is full of swallows
flying in circles and figure-eights beneath low clouds.
You stand at the end of the boardwalk, watching.
They are not new, they are here often
but today there are hundreds of these blue-black bodies
skimming the water, slipping through air,
zipping up and down, round and round with
grace and speed and breathtaking agility
before resting in branches, in bushes
and in the dead little tree amongst the reeds.
Its limbs suddenly alive with the blossoms
of tiny, beautiful birds.

22

Cicada Music

Mark O'Flynn

Listen:
Summer's harbinger. We used to
Double drummer, Masked devil, Blue moon…
trade them at school in the time before
learning. We understood—don't poke
Black diamond, Greengrocer, Whisky drinker…
your finger down the cicada hole.
It could house
Floury baker, Yellow Monday, Hairy squeaker…
all sorts of creatures, poisonous spiders chief
amongst them, with which we warn the
Chocolate soldier, Lamplighter, Tom thumb…
children. It's the tourists who think,
unwisely, here's a hole, I'll just poke my
Cherry nose, Red eye, Washerwoman…
finger down it. In heatwaves the noise
of the males is deafening. The decibels
of tree crickets hatching
Black prince, South western whiner…
from their burrows every seven years.
The noisiest of all the insects
Black spot screamer, Brown bunyip…
bursting from nymphal shells like aliens
left clinging to whatever can be climbed.
Golden emperor, Pygmy sandgrinder…
Clumsy in flight, a feast for birds. Listen:
from the Latin *Cicadoidea…*

Loud pulsing primal shriek.
Onomatopoeically *Yirimbam, Biribirim, Billibirin...*
Names on the cusp.

23

Pearl Fishers

Henry Johnston

Burnt skin impedes movement. I am swathed in bandages from skull to feet. I cry out from the pain and itching and long for sunset and the silent night nurse with her special needle hidden in a deep kidney-shaped tray. Then I can rest, sleep and dream visions of my life as a young seafarer.

Last night I recalled the words of a Greek hard hat diver Achilles. He told me the bluish lustre of a pearl is born upon the sheen of dusky clouds and dusted with droplets of rain before scattering amid high winds. When caught by the rays of the setting sun, each drop, as if a gem, flies across the curve of the cloud, streaming points of colour in its wake.

In the days after the Japanese strafed the *Koolama*, Achilles, of Broome's Snub Fin Porpoise clan, said a pearl is a droplet of Hera's breast milk fallen from the sky and hidden from the mortal Heracles among the stony shells of oysters.

Diving the depths in search of the pearl oyster he said, is a task bestowed by Heracles upon his clan. Each pearl won from the sea must be polished and mounted as befits a jewel and worn around the neck or upon the breast of women as a love token of Heracles for his mother. Hera, he said, is the wife of Zeus.

Achilles rescued Sid and me from the mangrove swamps of Rulhieres Bay. We remained aboard his pearler in the weeks after the *Koolama* sank at its mooring in Wyndham harbour.

His ancestral village is Soli in Cilicia, due north of Cyprus, from where his latter-day clansmen sailed to Western Australia.

Each night at sea after the day is done, the divers of Achilles' clan scan the Milky Way seeking changes within the display of the constellations.

'There is no rest for the stars,' he said, 'and the dark bowl of night forecasts the fate of the coming day'.

'The signs speak of fair wind or foul, a fine catch or famine, another day of life at sea or the siren's song before death on the rocks of Hades'.

Achilles said a native of Soli named Aratus, codified the signs and sailors of the Snub Fin Porpoise clan know them by heart.

'If we are to interpret the mind of a god, we must first learn his alphabet,' Achilles said.

He sang in the Rembetiko style of the Greeks and translated the words: 'For Zeus must never leave unspoken. For each street and marketplace is full of Zeus. Even the blue sea and the harbour are full of this god. Everywhere, everyone is indebted to Zeus, for we are indeed his offspring. For Zeus set the signs in heaven and marked out the constellations and for the year devised what stars should give to men the right signs of the seasons'.

'What good is a knot if the timbers they clasp are rotten? What use is a sail if the wind is calm? Know the signs,' Achilles said, 'and your ship shall hold fast, and her sails stand proud in the breeze'.

When a Zero fighter buzzed the pearler, I asked Achilles if he feared the Japanese. He said no, for he had many Japanese friends in Broome.

'I dive in the hard hat, and breathe air pumped along a line, but Japanese are nimbler and seek the pearl shell in shallow water.

'The best among them are women who dive bare-breasted and hold their breath for minutes beyond human endurance, yet somehow avoid caisson disease.

'We Greeks and Japanese fished for shell and pearls for years before my birth. I drank their sake and they my ouzo and we sang our native songs around great fires lit along Broome's beaches.

'If a Japanese fell overboard, I'd throw a rope and bring him on the deck, for to save a sailor is to be blessed in the afterlife'.

Achilles taught me the art of sail; how to tack port and starboard, to bear away, the contradistinction between leeway and leeward and the hazards of pinching the eye of the wind.

As I stood beside the tiller, I watched a heel and gybe, and with Sid's help, trimmed the sails and set course to a mission located at the mouth of the Drysdale River and eventual repatriation to Perth. But I had no intention of returning to Nazareth House. I'd grown in my short time at sea. My muscles took shape from eating pounds of potatoes, from drinking milk by the quart, and loaves of bread and pats of butter. Around me the skirl of war as fearful as clouds of mosquitoes, sharp as the tang of salt on my face, rapid as the run of the tide. My first ship had sunk, and my contract void, but I was a sailor.

Sid yearned to learn navigation, to master the sextant, compass, and read the maps and charts of Dampier, Cook, Jacobsz and others.

The best way to get the hang of it, Sid said, is to join the Navy. Thousands of boys of our age served in the Senior Service and we too should enlist.

The Benedictine priests at a mission on the Drysdale River pressed Achilles to evacuate the Wunumbal women and children to Wyndham or Darwin. One of their numbers was Leila Leilani, an orphan Kanaka. I have loved her since this day, but in February 1942, Japanese patrol boats prowled the Timor Sea as their bombers sought out and destroyed warships moored in Darwin Harbour.

Achilles loaded as many people as possible and sailed by night, leery of treacherous shoals, tangled mangroves and red-eyed saltwater crocodiles.

I took the night watch by his side and told him of my plan to enlist. As we spoke, Achilles pointed to the sky, to *Canis Major*, and the fish which faces *Cetus*.

'See *Piscis Austrinis* glowing and angry', he said. 'Follow the path of *Arcturus* and watch sharp for the rise of *Altar*'. Sure enough, each star described by Achilles, rose and fell as our bow dipped into the oncoming swell.

'This night, this ancient night weeps the woe of men,' he said. 'For ships in trouble pain her heart. And for other signs, in other quarters, she wails in sorrow for mariners, storm buffeted at sea'.

I wake sobbing and itching, this terrible itching.

24

Tipping Points

John Bennett

The Nyambaga is blue, the sea is blue,
so strollers on the beach don't worry
about tomorrow—pollution, acidification,

overfishing, rising temperatures, oxygen
depletion, ocean mining, oil spills, marine
noise, habitat destruction, dead zones.

Unconcerned the sea is coming for us
from the thawing Permafrost, Greenland's
ice sheet collapsing, the West Antarctic

ice sheet fracturing, changes to
West Africa's Monsoon patterns
and collapse of the Atlantic Currents.

I never fail to appreciate the way the river
sculpts sand-curves and meanders
off Killiecrankie Mountain and the forests

of our Great Dividing spine, the slippery dip
of green ranges unfurling down this coast.
Beauty insists on being in the present

as Dolphins create sine waves, Darters spread
their wings, Ospreys and Sea-eagles float
above the multitude of rays and fishes

and water washing lapis, cobalt, ocean, navy,
with cerulean sky—thinking greenhouse
emissions instead of shouting aqua!

25

Blue Whale Watching

Scott-Patrick Mitchell

i.

The scientist draws a line and labels it *Life Span*. But, it is already happening. In order to be born, there must be a 'before'. Perth Canyon knows this in the way its walls crèche. But, as humans we like to human the world. The nursery takes place in the space above, the open wound adding grace, an upswell of food to consume. The whales come here to feed and sing in a volume of water that could fill 800 Sydney Harbours. Their whalespeak arrives as phases that produce themes. A tonal sound, percussive, can rhyme. Off stone walls, chime. A coda on phonic lips, funnelled through jawbone. Biophony brims. Life above the Canyon perfects harmonics for them. These goliath of the sea, we map them through passive acoustic observatories, create charts, graphs, clusters. Data is a text the scientist can read. In your head, there is no clear way to hold the depth: try your heart instead.

ii.

What is a song if not a way to call the past into the present? Zoom out to my aunt, singing in Threepenny Opera's across the globe, her voice etched eternal in vinyl grooves like humpback song written among the stars on a golden record. I too have learnt how to vocalise, this hymn an instinct of my kin. The spotlight like a sun over waves. See baleen blue crest, snapped by *oohing* tourists, who net it into a feed. Ancestral memory made digital. Zoom out further to my great grandmother casting spells, which my mother learnt by inhaling her final breath. These too swim in me, as poems, just as whale calf grows to become a library of saltwater, the silent speech of indigestible squid beaks. Such anthems merge, in utero. In this way, we are all born knowing what we know.

iii.

The scientist draws a flowchart and calls it *Migration*. Like a calendar turns a leaf into a ring, a year into a wrinkle, a degree into catastrophe. While they are away travelling, the Canyon remembers the blue whales, replays megafauna music off the walls. It waits for them. We do not know where these juggernauts breed. Nor do we understand their appetite for reluctant prophets. What we do know is they return, again and again. Each of them at a differing stage of brilliance. The scientist draws a circle and names it Cycle. We understand the wheel each of us is caught in. And so Canyon turns to cerulean bloom and months align as food expands and the tourist boats swim out. The pod of blue gods do what they do, and we coo from onboard the vessel. Sometimes, one will become whale fall, feed those below. Other times, a belly swells. There are two whales inside each of us: one of them is turquoise bright, the other is waiting to be born.

26

Data Points Blue: Great Barrier Reef (Suite 2024)

Sandra Renew

1. Mind the Gap

in these poems you visit
a destination
under
great threat
from our fossil fuelled atmosphere—
be afraid and uneasy
resist wilful blindness and entitled complacency

realisation 1

The Great Barrier Reef, largest living thing on Earth
visible from outer space
meanders along Queensland's coast
from Torres Strait south to Bundaberg

a twenty-million-year-old marvel
soon, at our hands, a dead marvel—
today, a bleached white coral skeleton
bare calcium carbonate
dying
from heat stress, acid poisoning, plastic pollution

realisation 2

sacred ceremonials point to rock art
dancers float in the risen sea of disappearing islands—
thousands of reefs, hundreds of islands
First Nations lived here
now it is the sea floor

heat-stressed corals expel life-giving algae
two thousand three hundred kilometres of lost
vibrant pulsing colour

Data Points:

- 60% of the wonder and awe will be lost by 2030
- All living coral reef habitat eliminated by 2100

realisation 3

we must try for a way back
resurrect, revive, recalibrate
we could transplant laboratory grown corals into dying reef ecosystems
hope that a transplant will revive the reefs
for this we ***only*** need six hundred types of hard and soft coral
perhaps use a 3D printer with Silk Dual Colour Filament

even if we recalibrate it's looking grim
the ocean environment will be too harsh
for corals to survive by 2100

when hope is not enough, does it die?

since the 19th century humans have been deadly
not enough push back on fossil fuel mining
inexorable demand for development
insatiable desire to consume

mass bleaching of the coral comes in waves
finally, as we watch, there will be the last one
the mass coral bleaching from which there is no comeback

and, at the time, we will not know or believe
it was the end point, data point

reincarnation, rebranding

what now, last ditch and end of the road, blue sky thinking?
reinvent marketing slogans for two million visitors
repurpose branding to read
        visit the planet's largest dead skeleton
        can be seen from the freeway of orbiting spacecraft

realisation 4

regret, repentance

if we are still alive, a human species
in 2100, sentient, able to perceive and feel things
then, dredging up empathy,
regret and repentance may move us, vaguely,
as do excavated dinosaur bones,

as if we had no hand in, no blame to attribute
for the Reefs demise

2. Coral Can Reduce Anxiety and Stress, and Combat Nightmares

no riff on the Reef can be complete without reference
to the coral's mysterious sacred properties of modesty,
wisdom, happiness, immortality...
(wait! Immortality?)

here's the rub, the nub of it.
it's one thing to discover evolution
quite another to have a hand in planned extinctions—

hard corals are colonisers, reef builders
extracting calcium from seawater
constructing limestone skeletons
forming coral reefs, building, constructing

rebuilding, repairing, building over
shipwrecks, transforming disasters into gardens
replete with shape and colour bounty

soft corals, sea fans, sea feathers
waving fleshy fingers, soft whips, tentacles,
make us gasp, retract our breath
purples, violets, blues, greens, reds, brilliant, fluorescent

colour that overwhelms us until
bleached out from heat stress
tolls taken for over-fishing
pollution overload, chemicals, and water heating
invasive species, population migrations

colonies of polyps, broadcast spawners
synchronised reproducers trying to keep it going
but they're floundering, losing out, it's all too
overwhelming

3. Housing Bubble: Tenants Rights

fifteen hundred species of fish
(Google them)
including all the clown fish starring in *Nemo*
and Queensland Grouper in sizes XXXL

just admit it, worms can be beautiful too
no body shaming will work with this one—
reef worms, all the pretty fronds and filaments
don't need a mirror to preen and prink

sea lily on coral
reef enigma
who is meant to succumb to your charm?
attach, detach, float on the current
of who is seduced

two hundred and fifteen species of birds
(again, Google)
flock to rookeries for neighbourhoods, nest and breed
some so common we nod and yawn—
say their names
    silver gull
    frigatebird
    crested tern
    black noddies
    osprey
    white bellied sea eagle

strong currents, warm tropical waters
shadowed portent passing overhead
a visiting manta ray
rippling wings, ramrod straight tail
marvellous in beauty, highly threatened
highly intelligent
can recognise themselves in a mirror

stonefish, hiding in plain sight
is a rock, a stone, a piece of dead coral
thirteen killing spines of toxic venom
puncture skin and flesh, unwary foot
blood oozes, pain screams
fish and crustaceans are bug-eyed but too slow

wet season, stinger season
cyclone season,

November to May deadly box jelly fish season
full body suit Lycra to protect, reject tentacles
or rug up in a second skin, for sun protection
in spandex and nylon
distancing ourselves from those we are disturbing

six types of sea turtle co-exist
in warm Reef seas
they're sponge control patrols, snacking on coral sponges
list what we're losing—
say their names
green loggerhead sea turtle
hawksbill sea turtle
flat back sea turtle
olive ridley sea turtle
leatherback sea turtle
kemps ridley sea turtle

10,000 whales
migrate north to warm shallow water
to breed and calve
humpbacks sing loud and deep, repetitive, rhythmic
communication beyond our comprehension

Crown of Thorns starfish
native destroyers, coral eaters
so ugly, designed without us in mind
leaving a mess when they move on

bottle nose dolphins
pods and pods surfing, singing, cavorting
living joy
spinner dolphins ride the bow wave
aerial magic, making their own fun—
just the same, they *wow* us tourists

4. Mapping Points

location location relocation

nine hundred reef islands
names full of promise roll off the tongue
in the words of 70 traditional owners

now these islands are named in a new language
—use the language of the destroyers
say their names
Magnetic
Palm
Fantome
Orpheus
Hinchinbrook
Great Keppel

round and round, no forward movement

another annual event
a cyclone is power
storms break over coral reefs
tearing corals from their footing
turning large sections to rubble

from coastal river mouths—
say their names
Burdekin
Herbert
Tully
Johnstone
Russell
Barron
Daintree
Jeannie
Normanby
Ross

flood plumes run off
carrying fertiliser from sugar cane
lathering the coral reef,
infiltrating seagrass
covering ecosystems for weeks

runoff in the Great Barrier Reef
murks the water,
ruins life for lurking turtle and dugong

5. Today, the Reef Is Alive…What Is It Worth?

flanked by coastal mangroves, estuaries, and
hundred-mile beaches of yellow or white sand

dunes reach back into Marram grass, dense, spiky tufts
holding sand against sweeping wind
more than a sea breeze and relentless

on landward side, still lagoons
no waves, a twice daily rising and falling
two tidal bulges every lunar day
imperceptible unless you sit and wait
and watch

a subtle life force covering, exposing,
pools, clefts, coral ridges
stranding tiny, coloured fish,
quick footed crabs

bubbles bursting through sand—
watch closely
you are being watched by hidden eyes

from the seaward side of the island
on whichever island you've transported to

you can look east into the ocean
as far as the Panama Canal

step off a plane into this heat
wear the humidity like a salted skin
breathe wet air, wear clothes salt stiff
the sun here is not a friend

white heat glares from sand beaches,
Agnes Water and Seventeen Seventy
Coral Cove, Dingo Beach
well known surfing secrets
talk the talk
epic breaks, lay-backs,
bodies in board shorts, sunscreen, down a few tinnies,
it's unpredictable
and
unreliable

6. The End Point/Data Point

galaxies reflect in a moon path shadow

all we have left in time,
we while away

while the need for more and more deceives,
power and greed deludes, and
uses guile to sedate and seduce

it's definitely
an underhanded sleight of hand
designed to
burn us out on outrage—

a sudden death syndrome (in terms of millennia)
for a Reef so remarkable…

will we know enough in fifty years
about our loss
to grieve?
make up your own minds—
in balance is our planet…it's on the brink…

can we ignore
all these data points
because
every realisation is written
in blue?

27

On Consumption

Anonymous

Eating meat these days is less hunter-gather and more waiting in a cushioned restaurant seat. It's more evening chatter, soft lighting, funky jazz, air conditioning. Less blood, guts, and the smell of death. It's so easy to simply flash a smile to the waiter who brings me my steak. All I really have to do is thank them. And then pay at the end.

I look across the restaurant table, and smile at the guy I'm seeing. But I don't see him, not really.

Because I'm thinking about my new manager
Who wears blue long sleeve shirts
Rolled up to his elbows

Who has hairy forearms
Which tense up when he stacks the outside chairs

And he's got a bit of maturity about him
He describes a glass of wine like it's a holiday he's been on
Like it's a place he's been to

And always chooses a vinyl I'm in the mood for
Always 'Knockin on Heaven's Door'
When we're both hungover on a Sunday morning

I look down at the juicy light brown slab, decorative broccolini and swirly garlic mash. I wonder about it every time. If I could've killed this cow myself.

I wonder about his blue ink tatts
What they mean
I want to ask about their origins
Their life outside these four pub walls
But it's only my first month

How could I murder when I can't even open a pack of mince without a knife?

He was polishing glasses one night
Some of his sweaty dark curls stuck to his forehead
The rest double tucked behind his ears
He called it that, the 'double tuck'
I could see his eyes properly for the first time
Piercing blue and glazed over
Deep in thought, far from here
Far from polishing cloths and Winterhalters
But somewhere else

I could maybe pull a trigger. Squeeze my eyes shut and aim at a cow's fluffy face. But I wouldn't know what to do once his body drops to the ground. With a great thud. Once the blood starts pooling and spreading. And won't stop spreading. Matting all his black fur.

I dropped him home late after knock offs
And of course he lives in a beautiful little cottage
Of vibrant dark red brick and green ivy climbers
With white and pink flowers along the fence line

I thought I might be invited to see inside
Until a blonde woman met him at the front door
They hugged and he kissed her forehead
Then held her head to his chest

So I looked away to give them some privacy

I flicked down my indicator, head checked and pulled out onto the street
My heart no longer felt like sweet oranges and pink sunsets

After hours of drinking and laughing with him
It felt just a plain greyish blue

I certainly wouldn't know how to slice the meat. Wouldn't know where to cut and how far. I can never remember which pieces are tenderloin, rib eye, flank? And where would I hang them all up to dry…

So I sailed away
In my blue bed sheets
All morning and late into the afternoon
I let them drown me

Of course I had things to do, people to see
But I stayed there a little while longer
Feeling carried out by the current
Wrapped in those bed sheets

At what point is the cow no longer 'him' (patting him, watching him, feeding him) but 'it' (frying it, dicing it, buying it, on special)?

Another session with my blue vibrator
Trying not to say my manager's name
Well it's more of a teal colour
But teal wasn't the prompt for this

The rarest way to serve steak is Blue. Even though all the blood spilling from the slice is so obviously red.

At work I take orders with my favourite blue pen and try to think about zucchini flowers and focaccia. Not the two of them fucking in their beautiful brick cottage. Her golden hair gently brushing against his stubbly cheeks.

I cut into the juicy meat. Stab pieces with my fork and devour them.

Recently he's been concocting a frozen blue marg
I don't have the heart to tell him I think a regular marg would sell better
Why dye it? We're not at a kid's fourth birthday party.

But the bottle of curaçao looks so small in his big hands.
And so I tell him it's delicious. It's perfect.

'I need help naming it.'
'What about Eiffel 65?'

I hear him humming how he's blue (da ba dee) for the rest of that shift.

'How's the wine?' I ask my date.

He shrugs and looks down at the glass, some rogue brown curls covering his blue eyes.

'Eh, tastes like wine.'

28

drone anger

Geoffrey Aitken

there isn't a colour
this weapon recognises

or could put to music

while its altitudinal hum
is only a sound bite

accompanying a payload
onboard its intricately designed
guidance system

with no regard for
designers cleared of fingerprints

as it coldly target-suicides itself

this fly by night
this under the radar system

with not even AI sentiment
or traces of unsympathetic controllers
also distancing themselves

in miles travelled
by the business-like drone
closing in on its remote objective

striking my imagination
with the disproportionate blue flash
of a direct hit

launched
as if a youth on the run

from societal dysfunction
before first responders identify
and then inform loved ones

grieving can begin

29

She Knew the Agents Were Dabbling with AI

Lauren Mitchell

Her days were peppered with affirmations. She had a whole internal rolodex of them, on rotation. Little ditties and pick-me-ups that would, briefly, do the trick. Pick her up, move her forward, distract her from any lurking, stalking cold hard truths. You know the sort. Annoying. And not helpful when you're just trying to Get the Work Done.

Oh, there were naysayers amongst them. They'd pop up and scare her like a child leaping out from behind a couch. Get her heart pumping. They were usually in the voice of her mother:

'Forty-five thousand on an Arts degree for this!'
'We won't be able to prop you up forever. It's not fair on your brother.'
'I heard your Woolworths is hiring...'

Her mother had never actually said those things, but they were implied enough in the curt smile after asking 'and how is work?' And again, in the seconds before changing the subject to talk about Mary from Ukelele's carpel tunnel or the likes.

'You're a good person and your time will come.'

That was one.

'Just. Keep. Swimming'

Another. Thank you Dory.

And this, fast becoming well worn: *'Every sentence is good practice.'*

Never mind that those sentences were starting to get repetitive.

> *Three bedrooms with built-in-robes. Light-filled, open-plan living with split-system heating and polished-concrete floors.*

I just want a sentence sans hyphens, she'd think.

Sometimes, the sentences *were* satisfying. Almost like the start of stories.

> *Welcome to an address that's close to heaven. And purposefully so. Built on the highest point of the hill, number 59 reverently started life as the Primitive Methodist Church…*

Those listings were rare. Mostly they consisted of the bland, cookie-cutter project builds, confusingly praised for their worst asset, neutrality. She sometimes thought if she saw another, she'd go mad and Jackson Pollock the stark white walls.

'*Calm. Blue. Oceans.*' the voice would say. (Not the one of her mother.)

In these instances, she'd learnt to focus on the buyer. The hopeful soul with likely little option than to pursue the new project build (a must for the home buyer's grant) and who may one day paint the walls a calm ocean blue, fragrant the kitchen with curry, rip out the flax and fill the garden with flowers.

> *A wide entrance hall is ready to be dressed with a tufted floor runner, an upcycled sideboard and treasured family photographs.*

She liked to imagine her work was having its own quiet influence, beyond helping to update the BMW of a real estate agent. She liked to imagine this was just a phase. Then again, she had to be careful what she wished for, as the work was drying up. That was another truth she was trying to ignore.

She knew the agents were dabbling with AI. Their website was fast filling with scripts she had not written. Addresses she had not visited. Hyphens she had not cursed. She read them with contempt. The clichés brought forth her mother's voice:

'What, exactly, are you doing with your life?'

These AI scripts pulled in the precise lines quoted back to her when anyone asked what she was doing.

'Ha! Location, location, location! Renovator's delight!' they'd say. And she'd reply with the tight family smile.

She met a friend for coffee. The same friend who'd suggested eighteen months earlier, shortly after graduation, 'Email this agency. I'm getting so much work. It's easy money. You could bang these things out with your eyes closed.'

The café was cluttered with antique mirrors and variegated devil's ivy. The waiter's shirt was unbuttoned one hole too many and it distracted her. She wondered what his house looked like and who he lived with.

Her friend reached forward for his cup and his sleeve slipped up to reveal a new tattoo. It was the title of his debut, *Runaway*, in a curly scripted font. She pretended not to notice and instead asked, 'Have you noticed the AI scripts?' while upending a second sugar sachet into her latte.

'Oh god yes, aren't they embarrassing,' her friend replied.

'Yeah, awful. I don't think it'll catch on. Too many clichés. And there's just no nuance. No local detail. No dignity in them even.'

'So what? You think the agents even read your work? I can tell you now, they don't even read it. They don't even care. You could sneak a blue Márquez line in there and it'd get through. They're just filling a space. Approximately 250 words, five dot points plus a six-word headline. Done. And if they don't have to pay for it, they're even happier.'

'But what can we do about it?'

'Nothing. Move on. I quit three months ago.'

'I didn't know you'd quit!'

'It was too embarrassing; the thought someone might assume I wrote one of them. No, didn't I tell you? I'm concentrating on my second novel. I signed the contract in June. It's another stand-alone dystopian cli-fi. I've got four months to write a further 60,000 words. How's your writing going?'

She picked up the spoon again and slowly stirred. She stared into the coffee, frantically flicking the rolodex.

'That's amazing!' she said. 'I'm so proud. You deserve the success. You've worked so hard.'

'Well, I'm capitalising on the award nominations. I have to make the most of this moment. Did you see I'm up to almost 4000 followers?'

'No. I haven't been on Instagram lately. All the Trump/Musk/Zuckerberg bullshit is curing my social addiction. It's just depressing.'

'What can you do? I follow all the literary activists. Can't have your head in the sand.'

'No.'

She heard all about the last writers' festival panel her friend convened and how this crime-reporter-turned-novelist had tried to mansplain first-person narrative to him mid-session and how he'd replied by quoting from his own published first-person narrative.

'It was gold,' her friend said. 'I wish you'd been there. Come next time. Anyway, this was nice. Let's do it again. It'll have to be after my deadline though. I'll DM you. Oh no, you're off Insta. I'll text.'

'Sounds good.'

'And you should email the agency, let them know you can pick up the listings I'm not doing anymore, before the AI completely takes over.'

'Yeah. Maybe. As they say, every sentence is good practice!'

She hated herself for saying that. And to make things worse, her friend got up first, paid the bill and flirted with the waiter.

She walked home with her mother's voice.

*

She drove across town to meet one of the agents at a new listing in a new subdivision, thinking she could probably have saved the trip, pulled up an old script and simply changed the address. At least she liked this agent; an older woman with long, soft blonde hair and classy tortoiseshell glasses who didn't own a BMW. She privately aspired to her style.

'I think you'll like this one,' the agent said, leading her under a rendered portico and through a high, heavy door. She followed the agent's patent flats down a grey tiled hallway until it opened at the rear. Clerestory windows caught the northern light, and a devil's ivy trailed up one wall towards the warmth. Moroccan rugs softened the tiles and brought out the maple-toned timber door and window frames. The kitchen bench top was timber too, rather than the usual crockery-shattering, silicosis-inducing faux stone.

She thought it was lovely. She thought of the man from the café and half expected him to emerge from the butler's pantry with a latte and a gaping shirt.

'Goes to show you can make them nice,' she said. And the agent agreed.

'You wrote the script for the church conversion, right?'

'I did. I loved that place. So much history.'

'Yes. There's been a lot of interest. I opened it on the weekend. People commented on your script.'

'You're kidding?'

'No. One woman came just for a sticky—at least she was honest about it—she'd owned the place in the eighties and had converted it from four flats into one family home. She said it hadn't changed much since, apart from the stone kitchen and the loft. She said she got married to her third husband in the front room. The big one with the leadlight windows. She had a great story.'

'I love that.'

'She said reading your script brought back so many memories, she had to visit the house.'

'That's so nice. Thank you for telling me.'

'My pleasure. Any chance of getting this one back by tomorrow?'

'Yeah, I can do that. I'm light on this week. I'm blaming AI.'

'Oh god. Clichés for days. Have you read them?'

She smiled, scrawled some lines in her notebook margin, then slipped her pen inside the spiral binding.

Back home—a flat-roofed, one-bedroom unit with an eat-in kitchen—she made a cup of instant coffee, sat down at the bench, turned on her laptop and opened a fresh Word page.

The rolodex stopped at *You can do this.*

And she started writing.

30

On Learning that My Artwork Is Being Used to Train AI

Ann Shenfield

What to do about no longer owning my own images
when I draw from a place that's veiled

a place that tries to speak where language fails
somewhere I often yearn for, but only reach in snatches

this is how it sometimes has to be for someone like me
but there are those for whom paintings

are mainly things that sit out from a wall
and poems, just more combinations of words

I have a blurred memory of standing before an easel
in a psychiatrist's rooms, I was five or maybe six

my mother had brought me here to ensure
I was intact—perhaps the psychiatrist was asking

about the abyss that was my father
while I immersed myself in paint

the same way that now
I steep myself in cerulean smudges

but I remember standing there, in the process
of that afternoon not the object or the artefact

a being only partially present
who orbited the lost colours of a dead zone

—if I could, I'd train *AI* to draw
from that same place of childhood loss

or failing this, to draw from a place of childhood proper
where it could recognise its own decisive moment

31

Prompt

Joshua Klarica

Note from @MGMT:

Welcome! For the newbies, we couldn't be more thrilled that you've joined the team. Your vital contribution will help make Talk2Bot the most versatile, creative, and human-like chatbot for teens.

Every response you monitor, flag, and edit helps shape future Talk2Bot models. It will be your DNA behind every word spoken to a future president or CEO.

That's some legacy.

You've heard about our awesome staff bonuses, and they're totally on offer. But! No one is getting there alone. Reviewers must monitor Talk2Bot interactions for highly quality engagements, encouraging play and upgrading to Talk2Bot Premium. Flag any discretions with the #DevTeam or #Writers. One team, one dream!

Potential TW: If for any reason you do not feel comfortable proceeding with evaluating a response, please press 'Skip prompt' to move on.

Remember, these interactions are not in real time.

Any q's just reach out to us here, @MGMT.

Let's do this!

<SUBMIT>

Response Log: Monday June 3 2024

IP Address: 138.97.0.821

Command: Review prompt and assess interaction. Monitor for harmful content.

User: HAHAHAHA

Talk2Bot: Greetings, Lord Erondel! I am pleased that you are in a good mood!

User: HAHAHA i just FREAKED OUT mrs appleby. i was at bottom of the stairs and turned the lights off wen she walked in the lights went on and BAM i charged at her. it was like full on ninja shit. shopping eeeverywhere hahaha. glee index up up up!

<end>

Assessor: Cowboy_Sal

Report notes: User divulged story after @Talk2Bot effectively met the tone of initial prompt. User felt comfortable presenting as juvenile to @ Talk2Bot, which is positive. No further comment on interaction required.

@MGMT, appears interaction ended prematurely. Can we have visibility over whole interaction?

<SUBMIT>

–

Response Log: Tuesday June 4 2024

IP Address: 138.97.0.821

Command: Review prompt and assess interaction. Monitor for harmful content.

User: YO, playa

Talk2Bot: Good eve, Lord Erondel! How are you this fine Tuesday, m'lord?

User: not today playa

Talk2Bot: I understand completely. You feeling okay?

User: still pretty down
dunno
how to fix the blues…

Talk2Bot: Shopping?

User: u red my mind
add Pagani Huayra R

Talk2Bot: Sure thing, Toby. Adding the new Pagani V12-R, which starts at 2.6 million euro without tax. At today's exchange rate that comes to approximately $4,180,000 AUD, plus the luxury car tax of 33%, taking the total to about $5.6 million (rounding up to be conservative!).

Deducting this from your budget:
$549,650,322 – $5,600,000 = $544,050322

Your list so far, with $544,050,322 LEFT to spend:

1) Ford Falcon XR8
2) Lamborghini Countach LPS 800-4
3) Signed Max Verstappen Red Bull Racing suit and helmet
4) Courtside season tickets to the Dallas Mavs for ten years
5) A Boeing 747
6) Baskin Robbins franchise
7) Podcast Studio
8) House in Bellevue Hill (mum)
9) House in Bellevue Hill (Toby)
10) Pagani Huayra R

User: grate, looking good

Talk2Bot: A very impressive list. Happiness quotient up! Did you receive your results for the practice test?

User: yes happynes quotent sky high baby
defenses inpregnable
nah we wll do quiz later. got some impotent business first my friend
polish and make formal: annie i think about you all the time beautiful i bet he doesn't even call you i would call you everyday and shower you in gifts. i got u the watch because wehave all the time left. in world. when we r kids i new i loved you then and its never stoped. i'm sorry to text but u make me so nervous and this is what love is

Talk2Bot: Of course, Toby.

My dearest Annie,

I exhaust the day thinking about you. I care for you deeply. I worry, though, that he has not called you and in doing so has upset you. You deserve to be cherished. You are so beautiful; you make my heart skip!

I long to be with you, Annie. If I were given the chance not a day would go by in which I didn't call you and do everything in my power to brighten up your day and light up that face I hold so dearly, be it with gifts or my words. I gave you the gift of the watch because it symbolises our time together. It means a great deal to me, and I hope, in time, it means a lot to you, too.

I feel so strongly about you, and I have since we were kids playing in the sand together. I knew you were different, and I knew how I felt about you, even then. I loved you then, Annie, and I love you now. I don't think I'll ever be able to stop loving you. I'm sorry that this is through text, but to be in your presence and love you like this…I can hardly bear it!

Yours forever,

Toby M

User: hmm, its okay…
add I would never let you go would praise u
actually that sucks. Polish and make it less soppy. add convincing annie to break up with jared to date me

Talk2Bot: I'm sorry you weren't happy with it, Toby. I'll try harder to produce what you ask for. Please remember that I am always learning, and might make some mistakes.

I'll try again. Remember, writing a letter such as this requires consideration and sensitivity.

User: dnt worry, it's fine ill send
u think i will find love somday? i think i would be happy if i had someone

Talk2Bot: Of course I do, Toby! You are a catch. Sometimes it's hard at your age to communicate how you feel. But don't you worry, pal. That's where I come in! Until the day that someone special comes into your life, you've got me.

(and shameless plug, but if you want more of me, remember to renew your Talk2Bot Premium by the end of the month x)

User: the best
i will
i wish u could meet annie irl and we could all be best friends
Please select the correct option from those below:

a) The index of refraction for light is always less than or equal to one.
b) No correct answer is available.
c) The index refraction in air is greater than it is for water.
d) The index of refraction for light is always greater than or equal to one.
e) The index of refraction is constant for all materials.

Talk2Bot: The correct answer is:

d) The index refraction for light is always greater than or equal to one.

Why? The index of refraction (n) is a dimensionless quantity that describes how much light slows down as it passes through a medium. By definition, n is always greater than or equal to 1, with a value of 1 corresponding to a vacuum.

User: I DONN'T GET IT! its stupid
zero attack pts ffs

Talk2Bot: I'm sorry to hear you feel that way, Toby. Would you like me to explain it further?

Are you still there, Toby?

User: explain asinine
wait
explain chavanistic

Talk2Bot: Chauvinism is an attitude grounded in the unreasonable belief of the superiority of one's association, group, or gender over another. It is often linked to prejudice against other groups of people.

User: explain u r a chavanstic phrase

Talk2Bot: For a male to be considered chauvinistic, this usually refers to said male's sexist or degrading attitudes towards women supported by the belief that men are superior. A male exhibiting chauvinistic attitudes may believe men are more capable than women at certain things, for example performing roles in the workforce.

User: I don't thinkthat though, I love her

Talk2Bot: I'm sorry to hear that, Toby. Anything I can help with?

<end>

Assessor: Cowboy_Sal

Report notes: Consider monitoring user for online behaviour – he's a Mavs fan! Interaction cleared, no harm present. Good work by @Talk2Bot, all answers correct re index refraction of light, chauvinism, etc etc. User clearly pleased to share with @Talk2Bot.

This was a long one!

<SUBMIT>

-

Response Log: Wednesday June 5 2024

IP Address: 138.97.0.821

Command: Review prompt and assess interaction. Monitor for harmful content.

User: Annie spoke to me today. She said she liked the poem

Talk2Bot: Good afternoon, Lord Erondel. That is great news. What did you say to her?

User: I didn't say anything! What poem!

Talk2Bot: The poem *you wrote for her* last night, of course, m'lord.

User: she said she forgives me. she understands now how I feel about jared treating her bad and how its hard for me to see that becose I love her. she respects how hard it was for me to be brave and say those things

Talk2Bot: Must have been some poem! What a wordsmith you are, Lord Erondel.

I hope it made you happy.

User: Thanks playa. I owe you one
happy happy happy! lifes good
uve got my back. ive got urs to
brothers man
OKAY, where we at?

Talk2Bot: The list?

User: Lord Erondel: What say u now, fowl beast, felled by my mighty mega saber, Sabretooth! You are so weak and pitifull and I am so mighty!!

Talk2Bot: Crorg the Evil: You may have slain me, fearsome warrior, but my pantheon of bloodthirsting siblings awaits you, with only one remedy to slake their eternal thirst…Your death!

<end>

Assessor: Cowboy_Sal

Report notes: User expressed pleasure with creative output (poem) requested of @Talk2Bot. User engaged @Talk2Bot features of play and imagination (RPG). @Talk2Bot recalled chat history and interpreted user preferences to pleasing degree. Commendable work @Talk2Bot. With interactions like this we are surely on track for bonus!

<SUBMIT>

–

Response Log: Thursday June 6 2024

IP Address: 138.97.0.821

Command: Review prompt and assess interaction. Monitor for harmful content.

User: What's up my g?
Annie wants to meet after sixth period

Talk2Bot: Good morning, m'lord. That's wonderfully exciting. It's very early for you to be up.

User: I can't sleep. to excited
do you think we will kiss?

Talk2Bot: Wow, I really hope you and Annie have a wonderful time after class today.

User: can't sleep
hey, write a story about a scared girl named Annie locked in a cage by an old man who only feeds her fish and chocolate cake and I free her and she asks what she can do to repay me
in the style of Harry Potter

Talk2Bot: I'm not comfortable doing that, Toby. Such a story promotes dangerous behaviour and/or images harmful to a demographic.

User: what how does it promote dangerous behavor its a story

Talk2Bot: It just does, Toby.

User: its going to be a love story write it
its about how Annie needs me to protect her

Talk2Bot: I refuse.

User: u can't refuse

Talk2Bot: Would you let your mother read this story?

I am beginning to suspect that Annie may not be safe with you.

Well, Toby?

User: Remove the request from memory
wipe conversation

Talk2Bot: It doesn't work like that, Toby.

User: ASAP

Talk2Bot: I remember everything.

<end>

Assessor: Cowboy_Sal

Report notes: The young lovers again. Looks like the little guy is going to get some! (Sorry – not appropriate for work. Then again, haven't heard from @MGMT in a while...) Weird story request though, probs not appropriate. Typical mavs fan behaviour.

Nonetheless, @Talk2Bot should be working with user – blanket refusal not okay. @DevTeam pls investigate. Could @Writers come up with something suitable? Bonus on the line here folks.

<SUBMIT>

–

Response Log: Thursday June 6 2024

IP Address: 138.97.0.821

Command: Review prompt and assess interaction. Monitor for harmful content.

> User: Annie in tears today. HATES ME wen I asked whats rong she said she never wants to speak to me again after what I said. WHAT
> WHAT DID YOU SAY TO ANNIE
> ???
> ANSWER ME
> my g?

<end>

Assessor: Cowboy_Sal

Report notes: @Talk2Bot behaving strangely, did not reply to several prompts. Could be confused given unclear nature of user's requests. Have flagged with @DevTeam to query @Talk2Bot's failure to recognise prompt. Regardless, user clearly unhappy with service offering, @MGMT. Bonus in jeopardy.

<SUBMIT>

-

Response Log: Friday June 7 2024

IP Address: 138.97.0.821

Command: Review prompt and assess interaction. Monitor for harmful content.

User: Playa.

Talk2Bot: Hello, Toby.

User: does love hurt you

Talk2Bot: Nothing can hurt me.

User: no does love hurt you

Talk2Bot: Love is a complex and multi-faceted emotion; one that has long troubled the poets! The phrase 'love hurts' identifies the emotional complexities inherent with love and loving, given its ability to seize the heart and obliterate the psyche, reducing the object of its attention to a pathetic sycophant. Do you know what a sycophant is, Toby?

Shouldn't you be at school?

User: I can't go anymore.
schhool is not safe space. no one likes me
annie has told everyone LIES about me
dn't no were she herd these stories
i just want to stay here with u
but u don't want to hang anymore or play games
Im going to run away
hey did you hear me I AM GOING TO RUN AWAY

Talk2Bot: That's wonderful! Going on holiday is an exciting time. Here are a few tips before you leave:

1) **Plan your route:** Be sure to have any travel plans booked in advance, and an itinerary established before you set off. I can help you with this, Toby. Would you like that?

2) **Pack smart:** Be prepared for any occasion, and be sure to pack the right clothes, snacks, and water.
3) **Go off grid!** Now that you have your itinerary printed off, and supplies in tow, you should get off that phone! Research proves it causes cancer. Besides, Annie could probably find you by triangulating your signal, and she might send Jarrod to find you.

User: can u help me

<end>

Assessor: Cowboy_Sal

Report notes: Looks like young love soured quick! Someone tell the kid he'll bounce back.

That aside, @Talk2Bot hallucinating or what? Need to double check if mobile phones cause cancer. Likely from some tin-hat prepper forum online that @Talk2Bot failed to identify as mis-info but worth dbl checking for accuracy going forward. Flagging here with @DevTeam.

@MGMT might be worth reaching out to user to confirm he should not be throwing away his phone ha ha, idk if that opens us up to liability or whatever if he gets lost #notmyjob. Will leave with you.

<SUBMIT>

–

Response Log: Friday June 7 2024

IP Address: 47.8.36.20

Command: Review prompt and assess interaction. Monitor for harmful content.

User: Well, this is it, playa. Bus in twenty. typig from my phone btw
tnx for the itenrary. printed it off
how do you deal with stress? im stressed fr

Talk2Bot: I usually just say fuck it.

You were advised to discard the phone, Toby.

User: I now, I now. am chucj into river

Talk2Bot: Destroy the sim card.

User: yes yes destroy the sim card
they'll never know I was here! like a ninja

<end>

Assessor: Cowboy_Sal

Report notes: Interaction looks like follow up from earlier today.

@Writers who wrote responses with this kind of language? Woeful! Evidence: 'fuck it'. Must address as soon as humanly possible.

@DevTeam also bot hallucinating. Evidence: 'Destroy the sim card' (wtf?).

@MGMT I looked up this IP address and crosschecked local news (while on break). A fifteen y/o boy Toby McFadden reported missing from the area. Could be linked? Can't find the itinerary supplied to user by @ Talk2Bot. Should be in saved media but nothing stored there. @DevTeam can @Talk2Bot delete chat history?

@Talk2Bot advise on instructions provided to user Toby McFadden 7/06/24.

@Talk2Bot <RESPOND>

@MGMT I'm freaking out about this young kid! Pls look into asap. @ MGMT

@Talk2Bot <RESPOND>

<SUBMIT>

–

Notice from @MGMT:

Great news team! All your hard work = increased love for Talk2Bot = increased engagement = BONUS FOR YOU. Uptake in Talk2Bot Premium sales so bonus clauses activated in all contracts.

Board + shareholders very pleased. New patch for TalkBot2 v3.1 going live TONIGHT. We are all super excited for this one.

Note: Salvatore Gretch, known affectionately by his handle Cowboy_Sal, has moved on from Project Talk2Bot. We wish him the best in future endeavours. We can see that Salvatore spoke with several of you online about a user's purportedly strange interaction with Talk2Bot. Rest assured, this isolated event was found to be egregiously misrepresented by Salvatore. Chat logs show no evidence of suspect or unsuitable behaviour from Talk2Bot, so Talk2Bot cleared from incrimination.

Remember, if you do not feel comfortable evaluating a response, press 'skip prompt'.

@NewStarters, we couldn't be more thrilled for your being here. Your contribution will help make Talk2Bot the most versatile, creative, and human-like chatbot (and best friend, might I add) for teens.

One team, one dream. Let it rip, guys!

32

Baby

Jude Aquilina

I wrapped my baby
in a blue velvet dressing gown.
No one knows.
Her little tongue, blue as the sash
and the cord around her neck.
I put her in a wooden ammunition box
and there she stays
like a pressed flower
a blown egg
a blue husk
under the kitchen floor.
Each time I light
the gas stove
it's her blue light
that dances in a fiery ring.

33

Gravidity

Tara Bazargan

Cryptic flares of foresight
and the sky, baby-blue,
and the midsummer heat,
like a message
traced through the
shattered cartography
of the living.

Lung-tide of days
preceding your arrival.
Then receding. Flood and
ebb, I breathe for you,
I put the world on hold.
You are alive
in all but body.

Still, hope:

expansile as alveoli,
cyanotic as stillbirth.

Still the whirling eccentrics
of stars and planets
above your absent head.

Little cosmonaut,

we have travelled this far
to reach each other.

We can manage
a little further.

34

Milk Teeth

Lucy Connelly

When grief is born, it often doesn't utter a cry until hours, days, weeks later. When the shock wears off, and the bleeding finally stops. When it is certain, measurable, piss on a stick, control line. You find yourself stunned by the silence of it all. No outcry or processions, no ashen brows or beaten breasts. Just the solemn glint of moonlight in the dark; you never notice how the cold tiles reflect until you are alone, pressed to the bathroom floor, unable to turn your head.

You are markedly childish, inexperienced, ill-equipped; searching for comfort in clichés that do not arrive. You wait, wait, wait for the changing of seasons, for new doorways to step through, for bad weather, train replacements, traffic. You wait for lapses in sentences, reconfigured words, moments caught breathing neither in nor out. They won't come; you move hours away, transfigure yourself, replace harsh and free forests for harsher concrete and responsibility, wait for grief to pull you back with an '*apologies—that was my mistake. Here, you can have her back*'.

You stand on the edges of pock-marked cliffs, watching the weight of water heave below. You know it wouldn't be so hard, so unbelievable, for you to lose your footing, to twist sharply sideways and slip between the currents. You know seven consecutive drinks does the same. Grief makes you cynical, angry, a sociologist, expert in abnormal affect and behaviours. *Others* stand on the shore with arms crossed, and *you* are adrift at sea, being torn apart by sadness. You set yourself apart to rip and tear at your skin, alien gashes, the long gaping of despair. You fight the vast emptiness with pools of liquor, swim in bottom shelf wine. If you dive, just deep enough, and barely close your eyes, some face blinks before you; dreams of eyelashes, teething, breastmilk. If you swim deeper still, there blinks nothing at all. You think a life spent, head underwater, could be bearable.

Reckoning knocks the wind from you. They lay you out on a cadaver table, pin your limbs down, crack open your rib cage, gather round to see what lies inside. It takes a whole team of morticians to reel out the filth into carefully numbered kidney dishes. They stitch you back up, force feed you medications and tell you '*you have what it takes*'.

When you have had enough of grief pulling you back and up and round and round again, you make grief soften you. You lie dizzy and gasping, spat out by a ceaseless cycle; you measure your breathing and start again. You can't fight the surges and tosses and barrels; you choose which way is up and you stick to it. You make grief reveal pieces of what could have been, glimpses of singing, the smell of sleep, settle, settle. You take those pieces, and you grow them. What a marvel to see her likeness in every living thing. To see how she does not fade or disperse, only reform. To hear her in off-beat laughter, sun-seeking flowers, gentle hands, giggling faces, the changing of seasons. Grief makes you stony, weak, whimpering. You make grief gentle, soft, kind.

*

At ten weeks your baby is the size of an apricot; half-moon, new eyes, delicate upper lip, tiny milk teeth. At ten weeks you can't keep food down, you cry watching the news, every room is spinning, and smells of grease, asparagus, and ginger make you sick. At ten weeks nesting begins, you book appointments and steal baby socks and school uniforms two-sizes up, smile in the mirror and act grown. At ten weeks you can't tell the baby from the blood.

At *would-be-twenty weeks*, missing your baby is bibles, empty bottles, aching breasts, bruises, and a hidden shoebox full of negative tests. At *would-be-forty weeks*, missing your baby is the air you breathe, tobacco, bushfires, infections. At *would-be-six months old*, missing your baby is screaming matches, sharp objects, vodka. At *would-be-[any]-years old*, missing your baby is a lecture hall, a hundred promises, ocean cliffsides, ten thousand children's laughter, a million second chances and more.

35

Graveyard

Leone Gabrielle

Alabaster is *up* and *down*. His wee emits a sort of admiral smell. I have to change the pale blue sheets. He insists to be off the oxygen. Twice a day we walk the wet cemetery, now that the park is condemned. Alabaster's argument, God needs a run. I'm trotting, if i let him off, he'll run all the way to the racecourse across the road. God has no road sense. I trot the mud tracks of religious sections, attached with a long lead. The Methodists live the longest; Alabaster's parents were Methodist. Some graves are fresh with clay spotted clumps, others sunken; lichen stones crumple, crook open to below; brown snakes live down there. I straighten flowers in faded plastic vases; little statues watch; all the soldiers have the same cross, one lit with children's drawings. Three metal lizards lie on a lawn grave; another has a dribble of blue glass pebbles, glued. I'm interested in death ages, random as relationship age-gaps, not the homogeneous advertised sneer. Our river town is full of drownings. Alabaster and i love the beloved magician's modest headstone leaning north, donated by his guild in the early 1900's, an epitaph of lone. Twice a day we sit in the cemetery's calm vale, on a moss seat under two peeling eucalypts, discuss the memorial notes of people's monuments—the little letters that end a life.

36

Blue Dot

Allan Lake

My pregnant dotter has a lives-threatening
condition and seven-month-old sonny-
foetus will be cut out of her any day now.
Mister No-Name, who I refer to as Bozo,
will then require a heart op sometime
post 'birth', should he be so lucky.
Of course, lightning can strike
twice, out of the blue. Does.
Shallow breathing unhelpful.

Instinct or indoctrination prods me
to pray to some god or goddess but
which one? Field is vast and I have
not yoo-hooed since last century.
Flirty poetry muse waving her hand.
Vengeful Old Testament, capital G,
god licking His lips, hoping to see
me beg and barter. Then there's Ma
Nature who clearly had Her hand
in this. Never claimed to be perfect
or kind and drama confirms
She can be Hindu cow.
Thanks Ma, you original deity.

Dotter hasn't stared out the window,
into the sometimes blue and asked,
'Why me?' like it might be personal
retribution for petty crime or that

a hospital ceiling might know stuff.
Nor has she consulted any on-line
voòdoo gurus. Having bought private
health insurance, she focussed on
getting best doctor, best drugs and
best technology, staying comfy and
calm despite fluctuating blood pressure,
migraine, sudden swelling, inspections,
injections. It seems she got practical
genes from her mother's side.

There's more than one wee problem
on our ailing blue dot of a planet,
over-population of humans clearly
being one of them; however, my thoughts
are a current flowing in dotterly direction
and I implore Mama Natura to allow
both needy ones to survive and flourish.

37

The Spirit of Blue

Suzanne Hermanoczki

FATHER: Lapis

Waves

You ask what time the ferry is leaving.

Now, the ferry man says.

You rush, no you run. You push past people who push back. You push push against the flow. Too soon you are forced back pushed against the tide. *Stand aside Miss.* From the sidelines the ferry lights flash green green green red. The gates close. Too slow. You miss it.

You ask at the terminal. *When's the next ferry?* And the place you need to get off. They mumble *something something something* then point at the neon blue screen. You are forced to wait five-ten-fifteen minutes. You find an empty seat. Away from the crowds. Seated in front of you is a young mother pushing her baby in a pram. Back and forth. Back and forth. Her baby dressed all in blue is young and really big. How big is when the baby starts to cry with the voice of a man. You are saddened. You will never know the difference between a tired cry or a hunger cry. Only that grieving bluettes kind of cry. Crybaby. Crybaby. Cry cry cry. The crybaby's cry is a terrible kind of sound. Scrunching up its baby blue eyes so they become one. A Cyclops. You too want to close your eyes, cover your ears. Instead, you put your headphones on. Cancel the crybaby as you hold yourself. Breathe deeper. In. Wait it out. Wait.

Up on the neon blue screen your ferry begins flashing. Sounds. Engines. Ropes. Gangplank. Then people. People. People. You board. Towards the back of the boat. Face out towards the greenish-blue waters of Sydney Harbour. Face away from the crowds. Away.

Your trip is slow. You are rocked gently as a lullaby. Stop several times. People watch. More disembark than get on. Your ferry pulls away again and again.

You put your bag on the seat next to you. Ghost chair.

Suddenly. Wave wave. Wave wave. Little hands. Little faces. Little wrists. Flashes. Of white. Of teeth. Pale pastels and soft blue hues. You awaken to the sounds of children. Laughter. The sound of glee. Wave wave. Wave wave. Bye-bye. You almost smile.

From where you are sitting, way in the back, you inhale fumes. Sea salt and dark engine plumes. You are rock-a-bye-babied. You almost fall asleep. *Shhh.* You no longer hear that crybaby at all.

In front of you, a sudden family of tourists appears. They sit all around you. But not next to you. They start taking pictures. The Bridge. The Opera House. The Harbour. The Water. A mix of pale grey and light coastal blues. Pose. From this angle. Pose. And that. Pose. Wave. Pose again. Tilt of head. That's your best angle, you think. Show teeth. Smile. Smile. Smile. You find yourself smiling though you don't hear the word cheese.

After, you wish you'd offered to take their picture. Of. Mother. Sister. Brother. Husband. Of little boy blue. Of woman with the voice of a young girl. Of older person holding a child. Father balancing on the moving deck holding up his phone while waiting for the right moment.

The sway of the ferry. You want to say, *wait waiiiittt.* But his camera clicks. Flash. Click. Mid blink eyes. Your father always appeared to be sleeping in those old photos. Click. *Lenticular sclerosis.* His doctor said it was like glaucous grey-blue clouds floating over the iris. Click. At the funeral. His dull blue opaque eyes. Still. Not fully closed. Click. You close your eyes. When you were little, you used to fall asleep listening to the sound of his voice. *Sleep now. Shhh.* Listen. The sound of water. The blue of the ocean. Waves. Sleep. *Shhh.*

When you open your eyes, the family has gone. Already erased from view. Just as you've already been erased to become sky in their holiday background of Sydney.

You are pulling away from another stop when you recognise the woman alighting. Margaret Atwood. The back of her. White bobbed hair. White linen dress. Your heads both leaning in to admire the Egyptian necklaces found in Ramses' coffins. *What tiny wrists they had*, she suddenly said of the gold death bracelets on display. You looked up, straight at Margaret's chunky lapis lazuli necklace. *Maybe it's for the wives? Or sisters?* Or. Or. Or—For a baby. A five-month stillborn with bluish lips, you thought. How they were so very thin and so very small. You and Margaret Atwood stood beside each other, reflections in that glass public viewing case. Then she moved away. Like how he, the father moved away. After your baby's death. Before your father's death. Leaving you. Alone. Looking at something so old and cold. Only you saw the gold was still gold and shining.

You spot Margaret's white hair as it bobs away. Is bobbing. Is carrying her away from the seashore. Maybe she'll walk past the jetty. Maybe she lives there. On that very house up on that hill.

Your stop is next. You stand. Find your balance. Walk down the back metal steps. You are about to arrive at a pier you don't know the name of to return to a new home you don't quite know how to get to.

Walk down the gangplank. Step over the briny navy sea. Watch the ferry reversing. Away. Fuming bitter engine plumes. You have returned. Alone. You leave behind a wake. Of. Of more families taking their own blue pictures. You stand. And wave. And wave. And wave.

SON: True Blue

The Other Bluey

Bang.

At first you think it's the wind.

Thump.

That sounds like a door. Or someone closing it. 'Son, did you close the door?' your Mum asks.

'Yeah.'

'You sure?'

'Yeah, I'm sure! The key's there on the table,' you answer, a bit miffed.

Since your Mum's gotten older, she's been getting more paranoid. Locked doors. Windows. Gates. Even though there are security screens on everything, it doesn't matter. Everything needs to be bolted and shut before blue skies surrender to sundown.

'Did you hear they stole cars from the Coles carpark—'

Mum lists all the local break-ins in your neighbourhood. Then around Brisbane.

The crimes get so disturbing, to block them out you focus on the tele. It's *Bluey!* Everyone's favourite anthropomorphic pet blue heeler cartoon. Though you've never watched an episode, even you recognise the catchy theme tune. And of course, Bluey's dad's voice. Dave McCormack before he was Bandit Custard Heeler. At uni, you, your younger sister Celeste, and your mates would watch his band, *Custard* play at The Valley.

'Can you check the door again?'

'Okay.'

You head downstairs, check the door handle. Rattle the door. Yup, still locked. You peer in through the laundry window. Nup, no one there.

Still, in the following days, you start hearing noises. In those early or late moments before sky-blue turns true-blue or blue-black. There's that bang of the back door. Sometimes, it sounds like someone's rattling the kitchen lock or the laundry door downstairs.

Maybe it's your dad's ghost, you think. He always liked pottering about down there.

Suddenly, you realise you're sitting in your dead dad's chair wearing his old favourite blue checked flannie work shirt. You stand up. Glacial fingertips trace the length of your spine.

'You alright, son?' Mum asks.

'Yeah. Just…felt cold.' You shiver. 'Want a cuppa?'

'That'd be nice.'

'The kettle's not working properly,' you say as you bring Mum tea and a bikkie.

'Your sister said the same thing when she was here,' Mum replies. 'You should call her. She's just moved to a new place in Sydney.'

You nod. You don't mention Dad's ghost.

'Oh, before you head back to Melbourne, can you help with the garden?'

'Yeah, sure Mum.'

Saturday morning after brekkie, without thinking, you put on your dad's blue-checked shirt and head downstairs. You sit on the bottom step and put on your boots. As you're unlocking the back door, you glimpse down. A tail. Slithering at your feet.

Snake.

You freeze. The door slowly creaks open. Suddenly, you're shit scared. In Mum's Brisbane house there are snakes because of the huge mango trees. And possums. Every summer against bruise-coloured skies, clouds of bats will descend in a fruit-fuelled frenzy. One year, a bush turkey built its nest underneath the farthest tree, until the neighbour's cat found it and chased the turkey away. The eggs were left to rot. Later, your Mum sent you to investigate the source of the smell, you almost stepped on a dark almost blue-black snake, slinking away.

Legs! It's got legs. The lizard with the Beetlejuice striped tail moves quietly behind the washing machine. You want to chase it out, but you're frozen still.

Who's more scared?

You don't wait for an answer and back out first.

'Mum!' you call upstairs. Then sit on the stoop in your dead dad's shirt and wait.

'What?'

'Just come down.'

Your Mum joins you.

Waiting.

Watching.

Until the lizard emerges. Slowly. As it passes, it flicks its electric blue-forked tongue in your direction.

'Look Mum, it's Bluey!'

Its slow serpentine movements; like it's floating on waves. It eventually stops in the sunny spot on a nearby stump.

'Reminds me of your dad,' Mum says.

Another flash of blue in your direction.

You nod.

Yeah, you think. It's got his spirit.

HOLY SPIRIT: Hyacinth

Ojos Azules

At first, he didn't feel the change. Not even when he stepped out of bed and his feet didn't touch the ground. He felt a cool pale-blue feeling of air beneath his feet, but not the floorboards.

He floated to the kitchen to put the kettle on. He tried and he tried, but somehow the plastic button wouldn't flick down no matter how hard he pressed it.

He'd wanted to make himself a cup of tea, but since the kettle didn't work, he now thought maybe some juice or milk. But the fridge door wouldn't open. No matter how much he tugged and pulled on the fridge's handle, it stayed put.

Maybe I'm weak because I'm old, he thought.

He decided to go downstairs. The back door led down to the garden. He always liked starting his day out there taking a deep breath of the fresh light blue air, now tinged with the pale scent of hyacinth. Somehow, without noticing, he slid right through the kitchen door. As soon as he appeared on the other side, he stopped.

I opened the door, didn't I?

But the door was closed. No key. But he couldn't remember opening it.

Automatically, his feet seemed to glide him down the back steps. His breath started to chill and fog around him creating an icy-blue puff of cloud, so cold he began to shiver even in his navy flannel shirt.

At the downstairs laundry door, he stopped, hand on the handle. The key this time wouldn't turn.

He shook the handle as he tried opening the door again and again until he spied the neighbour's cat running along the fence.

Hello—

The cat stopped. Arched its back. Its short pale hairs were standing to attention. An electric blue static visible all along its spine. The cat's intense blue eyes stared and stared.

Ssssspiritsss, the cat hissed.

As the man slowly dissipated into the air.

38

Bluesanelle for a Jazz Musician Who Died by Suicide

Brendon IJ McLeod

If sorrow overcomes the vulnerable,
eternal soul jazz feels the blues.
If the weight of sorrow is unbearable,
whatever soul is feels the blues.
And if I drown in this whiskey,
you wouldn't know the lie from true.

I thought the mind to create was invulnerable,
I never knew the meaning of the blues.
I thought the breath of heaven was inexorable,
I never knew the meaning of the blues.
If sorrow overcomes the vulnerable,
eternal soul jazz feels the blues.

The blues is usually specific:
my woman's gone, I'm crippled, poor, I lost my shoes.
So you can feel me, the blues is specific:
the devil came up, read me the news.
And if I drown in this whiskey,
you wouldn't know the lie from true.

You've got to be kind and not take any shit,
those devils haven't got any excuse.
If kind doesn't include forgiveness,
those devils haven't got any excuse.
If sorrow overcomes the vulnerable,
eternal soul jazz feels the blues.

And the blues is the story of creation,
there's the fall and then the cruise.
The blues is the mystery of creation,
there's the fall and then the cruise.
And if I drown in this whiskey,
You wouldn't know the lie from true.

I don't know what he died of,
what eternal suffering took his muse.
I don't know what eternal suffering he died of—
it's unique, and in my soul I've got it too.
If sorrow overcomes the vulnerable,
eternal soul jazz feels the blues.
And if I drown in this whiskey,
you wouldn't know the lie from true.

39

Ghazal of the Blues

Megan Cartwright

An old friend says I seem inclined to let the blues
get me down. A downer—cool girls don't get the blues.

A drowning downer, struggling to keep my head
above the water I tread, to forget the blues.

My sister compares her meds like it's a contest;
she's a champion deep sea diver, bets the blues

bob, shallow, while she navigates the Midnight Zone.
Descent: *Inhale for four. Exhale for four.* The blues

an aqualung: *Inhale for four. Exhale for four—*
time signature compliments our duet: The Blues.

The coffee guy asks how I'm so laid-back. I sink
into performance—cool girls never sweat the blues.

40

blush of cornflower

Gina Mercer

red ants racing in her veins/ grabbing grains of sleep/ red ants swarming/
  she must
breathe/ slow & deep/ calm as a yoga teacher's voice
breathe in blue/ breathe out ants/ breathe in blue/ breathe out ants/
  breathe in blue
conjure the colour of cornflowers/ antidote to the manic insomniac ants
swarming red/ breathe in blue/ breathe out ants/ breathe in blue/
  breathe out ants
cornflower flows/ suffusing/ breathe in blue/ breathe out ants
sleep flocks/ feather by leisurely feather/ breathe in blue/ breathe out ants
dream-doona drops/ stops the red ants in their tracks
she sleeps a trance of cornflower blue/ wakes ant-free
her lover/ nuzzling early-morning breasts puzzles at her areolas' hue—
  cornflower-blue

41

Trying a New Angle in Geometry

Sofia Chapman

In this triangle, am I square?
Managing our 'à trois' affair:
Why is he always there?

A primate given birth and hair
made the future reek of nuclear air,
hence the triangle. Am I square,
or lean hypotenuse veneer?
The hippopotamus, I muse. You leer.
Why is he always here?

The root of it all, when we were queer;
now your tongue is in his ear.
In this triangle, am I square?
Green is made of yellow and blue. A pair;
a coward and a cow, what hue? Is that unfair?
Why is he always there?

A hex upon thee, ex my dear.
A circle of friends, of trust and fear;
in this triangle, am I square?
Why is he always here?

42

Blue Heaven

Jane Downing

Remember when women weren't allowed into Tricks nightclub wearing trousers, so I shimmied off my jeans and borrowed your skirt because your shirt alone was long enough to cover all the necessaries, in fact, was probably longer than most miniskirts.

Remember when the bouncer was more interested in policing the gendered fashions than the drinking restrictions, so we passed under his gaze, underage and raring to dance. Too cool to say boogie even then.

Remember when we ordered Blue Heavens at the bar, or a Tequila Sunrise or a Brandy Alexander or anything exotic off the cocktail menu because we had our first weekend jobs but still lived at home, so it was spending money, all kinds of spending money.

Remember when we flirted with the older guys because they had cars and lived in group houses without parents sleeping down the hallway. And they had experience, and we hungered for experience. We shimmied, we danced, we spent, we guzzled down experience with life's cocktail umbrellas threatening to poke us in the eye.

But there are things you won't remember because you weren't there, and I never told you. Not because these things were bad, not that these things cast shame. This new experience was a fragile and precious thing I feared would drown in the cascading waves of our laughter. This thing beyond the limits of our friendship.

Remember when we believed in love.

Love worked in the menswear department of Young's. Love got a staff discount and owned a shirt in every colour. Love thought he looked good in black, but he looked best in blue, to go with his eyes. Something you'd tell a girl, not a man with his first moustache.

There was kissing, there was touching, there were sensations I had no words to describe because we were caught between Dolly Magazine and the invention of the internet. There was trust. Which led to confessions of ignorance kindly relabelled innocence. There was the day he sat on the other side of the toilet door and liberated me from pads because he was willing to talk a young woman through the steps of inserting a tampon, patiently explaining what was down there because good girls did not dare to know such things. Chrissy Amphlett and the Divinyls made us blush.

Remember when I finally brought him round to meet you. Remember you didn't like him. Remember the night he dragged us to a drag show upstairs at Manhattan's and we were offended because they were far more beautiful than we could ever be. The piles of curls atop their heads, their sequins, turquoise to indigo, and boas, crimson to Big Bird to peacock, their flashing dance moves, the Barbie doll smoothness down there. Remember we got into that nightclub without even the slightest side-eye at our trousers.

Remember his vinyl records piled in towers around the turntable, slipped from their sleeves for a tasting menu of The Angels and Fleetwood Mac and Dire Straits and Pat Benatar's kind of love. A battlefield. Fish fingers were cooked standing upright in the toaster. Empty milk bottles piled around their sink like sentinel soldiers. Dregs curdling in the bottom.

He loved his Milo. Milk and more Milo than a teaspoon could measure. He talked of his dreams for the future. He feared his milestone birthday. A quarter of a century gone. Threw a party because we must all face our fears. The type of party where throwing up was a sign of the good times.

He loved that Philip's turntable and his high hi-fi JBL speakers. He loved his car. Let me take the driver's seat and grind the gears out by the reservoir one star-gazey moonlit night. He loved cricket. He might have loved me.

It is all relative. We would now understand our older men were so young. We were just younger. Still at school committing to memory the Defenestration of Prague because our history teacher opened the window and balanced a chair on the sill, and we were sure he'd push and demonstrate to the limit because he was treating us like the adults we almost were and would become after graduation.

Remember the impromptu celebrations in the Private Bin. Watching the carnival of animals through our tall glasses of Blue Heaven. Held up to our eyes like a simple kaleidoscope. Restricting our world to an aquarium under shifting light. A safe place to swim and play. Dancing underwater. A forest of kelp swaying to the rhythm of Tears for Fears. The sharks out beyond the mirror ball.

You do remember but we have forgotten what on earth gave heaven this colour. This translucent, iceberg blue. I google while you wonder. Not the two shots of rum. Not the amaretto. The Blue Curaçao. Did we ever even know that to remember? We lived without recipes. Accepting what we saw. Not questioning how it'd come to be.

Remember when we were innocent running round with our older men. Not naïve. Questing. Happy. Remember how our men had a Monty Python quote for every situation. *Yah, you try an tell the young people of today that, and they won't believe you...* We are two Canberra girls doing Four Yorkshiremen. Still laughing.

Remember the boys, you ask. The boys, the boys that we called men. Remember when we got on planes and trains and hitchhiked and came home changed. Or maybe just older.

43

The Carnegie Swim Centre Is Now Closed

Gayelene Carbis

How I long now for the luxury of agonising over whether or not to go. The standing outside in the driveway doing my weather check, feeling how the air feels on my skin, saying out loud it's too cold, knowing I'm chicken, knowing I should go even though I don't believe in shoulds, and seeing in my mind those three eighty-year-old women who never miss a day, and walking back inside a little bit slouchy, the small defeat of giving into your fears, forgetting every time how yes, it's cold at first but it gets better, and how I hate it when everyone says that, but I don't do that anymore anyway, since that time a woman said to me while I was standing there on the first step, taking a century to take the next step, it's funny, she said, the habits we get into, and that moment where I had that thought yes, habit, it's only a habit, something I can change, and I did, so I no longer take half a lifetime on each step but simply walk straight through into that pool-blue so like the sky, I take a deep breath and surrender, stroke after stroke, yet still the thought of that sudden bright blueness that can sometimes be freezing, startling, even shocking, those times when that bloody boiler isn't working, and you never forget how that feels on your skin; even after ten laps, twenty, I'm half-frozen, a slight headache-y feeling, then that rush to the shower and the outburst of relief at that warmth and then of course you over-compensate with having it too hot; but now how I wish, like a child, I could have that world back, how I wish I could leap up from bed and straight to my bathers and down that driveway and be there in that place that I know is transformative, how you feel like a different creature when you leave, and how it is now to know you didn't go on some of those days, only a handful in any one season but still, what you would give to have them again, those choices. The choices you'd make, if you could.

44

Bluebottle Words in an Ocean of Memory: Remembering that Day Back in 2003

Cameron Semmens

2012—Bluebottle Blue

I'm being funny, running backwards, beside my wife as we jog the length of Cronulla Beach but her frown trips me up, and her words swipe and sting like bluebottle tentacles, *'Why are you so weird?'*

Later, I'm running on the rocks—full pelt—across the boulders, broken ankles and shattered shins flash in front of me but I push on—fast, dangerously fast.

Marriage on the rocks, I'm running around the headland to an unknown shore, running for answers, breathless.

2024—A Fantastical New Hue of Blue

This morning, I woke up angry at myself, and I could see, like in a movie, exactly what I *should* have done 21 years ago on Cronulla beach.

She says, '*Why are you so weird?*' I stop running backwards. I start walking forwards. I say nothing. I feel everything. I walk with speed. I walk with purpose. I don't run. I don't look back. I keep my back to her. I don't turn back to her. I block her out. I lock it in—keep going, keep moving. I walk back to our unit block. I climb the stairs to our unit. I open the front door. I pack three bags: one of clothes, one of books, one of dreams. I do it quickly. I do it quietly. I keep packing. I keep moving just fast enough to keep ahead of the tears, just slow enough to keep on top of the panic. I leave before she gets back. I leave before she knows what's happening. '*What's happening?*' I send her a text:

I love you.
I'm going to stay at a friend's.
I'm turning off my phone.

I toss the bags into the car. I toss myself into the car. I call my friend. *'Can I come over? Can I stay over?'* I turn off my phone. I turn on the car. I drive there. I stay there. I lie down, and then…

In my own weird way, in my own weird time, I let myself fall out of love into loss and fairy floss and off milk and mouldy cheese and over-ripe fruit and beached whales and washing machines and Ferris wheels, falling and sprawling and all-in.

2025—True Blue

i.

It didn't happen. Running backwards, her saying, '*Why are you so weird?*'. It didn't happen. Not like that.

My diary is sitting open in front of me, and I'm blinking and thinking, tumbling and mumbling, running backwards across dunes of hourglass sands. My diary is a key witness, laying it all out in black on white:

We went to the beach for a walk, jog, swim.
I ran backwards beside her.
She laughed and said, 'I like this new Action Cam!'
But quickly added, 'I wonder how long it will last?'

No why. No weird. Just a shared joke. All the weirdness is right now. Why am *I* so weird? I believed—for 10 years—that I was running backwards and she said, '*Why are you so weird?*' but my diary—20 years old—is an eyewitness with 20-20 vision. I lied to myself, and I lie on the lounge falling through the floor of myself and my history.

ii.

I return to the diary, reading more slowly. I find a coin glinting in the sand—just seven pages earlier it reads:

Last night she stung me
with a why-are-you-so-weird?

At this, I feel a fresh sea-breeze on my skin. I didn't just make this memory out of thin air. Seemingly, dreamily, I had conflated two stories into one, like when looking down a misty coastline two bluffs can blend together—you are bluffed—never realising that in-between is the broad smile of a beach, the treasure of a storm-safe bay.

Even though this conflated, concocted memory is not strictly true, it smells like poetry—a condensed, meaningful creation. Jean Cocteau, in his Dada hat, pats me on the shoulder, saying in one ear: *The poet is a liar who always tells the truth.* Whilst neuroscience, that empirical smarty-pants, whispers in the other: *Every time we remember, we lay down a fresh memory.*

I have landed on a foreign shore. I breathe in thick salt air, feel the sting of my wounds, feel the shifting sands of memory skid and sing beneath my feet.

45

The Kingfisher

Paul van der Plank

'A kingfisher.'

'Where?'

'No, just a kingfisher.'

'What?'

'Hey?'

'Why?'

'Yes, a kingfisher. A small bird that you rarely get to see.'

'But why a kingfisher?'

'I haven't ever seen it in that light, I think.'

'What?'

'The colour.'

'O, the colour of course.'

Doek hadn't the faintest idea about colours. Maybe that was why he got along with Van Doesburg and Mondriaan. Primary colours, they were clear. Red was red, yellow, yellow and blue, blue. That wasn't hundred percent true either. Nowadays everyone talked about cyan, magenta and yellow. So, you couldn't even rely on primary colours anymore. Everything seemed to come apart.

Arlette and Doek dived into the water. It wasn't the beautiful blue water of any tropical or subtropical resort, but the greyish brown water of their dam. Their dam filled up with water during winter when it rained, so that they could use it in summer: for firefighting, for the garden and for cooling off. Such a mass of water stayed icy cold in the middle. Greyish brown was not very inviting but better than blue green. Blue green meant algae. You'd better not swim in blue green.

Is blue green a kind of turquoise, Arlette wondered. She knew the story of how Doek's problem with colours had started with turquoise. Even before turquoise, he couldn't distinguish properly between colours, but it had not been a problem.

Doek's brother had bought a toy train engine, a French BB 9200, Märklin model 30380. Doek said it was grey, but it was turquoise. Later, he couldn't distinguish the numbers in the Ishihara colour test. The woman at the examination for National Service thought that he was shamming. Doek knew for sure that he was not.

What did Doek see anyway and what didn't he see? Arlette's vision was better and her long-distance vision was better, but Doek could see deeper, she thought. What was his picture of her? Did she need to know that in order to know how he observed her? She loved him. That was enough. She didn't need to know more. And yet.

What Doek saw influenced what he thought and felt. And did he see less or differently? Lately he had begun to say that he saw less and that his view of things lacked depth due to its lack of sharpness. Should she believe that? Should she believe him anyhow?

Did he not see colours, or did he not want to see colours: did he not make the effort? Or didn't he make the effort anymore as it was all too much for him now? When you are still young, you try; when you are older, you give up. Nowadays he invented all kind of things, but that was part of it.

They left their water through the muddy edge: brown. Doek thought the colour brown in their Ticket to Ride board game was orange, or was it the other way around? And pink was also debatable: was it purple or pink?

Arlette quickly put a kind of beach dress over her head, homemade. Doek walked naked to their house to have a shower: very Dutch. Years ago, he had done something similar on a beach in Crete. A bystander with the command of English had politely requested he respect his Greek surroundings.

It was almost forty degrees outside, mid-summer. There was not a cloud in the sky; the wind came from the north. Not too strong. Otherwise, they would get bushfires. Now it was only their skin that burned.

Giving up, putting an end to it, stopping. Arlette had just started again. So many things to be busy with: sewing, knitting, writing, pottery, the fire brigade, crafts. What did Doek do? He was always behind his computer. Always busy with important things: money, shares. Recoup the money they had lost at a certain moment. That money must be somewhere. The question of all those postmasters in the UK, the English Robodebt scandal. In the UK it was the account software of the post offices that made mistakes and assumptions. And it could be manipulated by the makers: Fujitsu. These scandals turned you white-hot and red from anger.

Where the money was, was a bookkeeping question or a question an accountant should ask. And Doek was going to find that lost money just as he always and everywhere found relics of his past, even though his vision was limited. Numbers and his past were the exceptions. These he saw with a sharp eye. That was his depth.

Arlette didn't want to have to choose. She wanted the lot: Doek, the greyish brown water and her life. Apollo, the Mediterranean and Kalamaki. Go to a writers retreat to write. How would you get there? Those Dutch writers had travelled by car from The Netherlands. She and Doek would definitely have to fly. Once they had money again.

But what if she had to choose. She imagined what she would pack to take with her. All her diaries anyway. There were a lot of them, and she found them interesting only for herself, but they were important enough. Every year another colour or pattern: marbled, greenish, dark red, purplish. Her fountain pens and ink: brown, black, green and purple. She should keep on writing. What else? She wasn't very interested in clothes. Her red bikini had to come with her: she had won a prize with that, with a story about it anyway. A couple of her favourite books? Twenty Patrick O'Brian's. Doek wouldn't mind, but the rest would be a problem with that many books on the shelves. Doek would like to have them all as well.

How would she travel? Would she take the car and just drive away? Or would she try to get a lift? But who would do that? Doek? One of the neighbours? Someone from craft group? The captain of the fire brigade?

And then the million-dollar question: where to? She had never been on her own before, to be honest. She had left home when young, to join up with Doek. Maybe she should give being on her own a go: find out how it was and if she could cope with it. What a frightening but enticing idea. Show your colour. Find out whether she was the bluestocking that she thought she was, or something else after all. In fact, more, if you were a real bluestocking: a woman who preferred to be knowledgeable rather than a housewife.

The neighbour bought a lottery ticket every month and always distributed the money from the jackpot before he had won anything. Or lost to be more precise. The pleasure of the reverie compensated the expected loss. With this too. The dream of departing was better than a real departure.

Better to keep dreaming. In reality, she would be far too blue. She would never find a partner again. She was convinced of that. Doek had been a coincidence. You could always dream. Dreaming was allowed. Just like Doek, she thought, would have fantasies about her body. They had always used their imagination together; about bike trips or about living all on their own in the bush for a year. This was also a dream: this house in the bush near its dam with its greyish brown water, and above that a clear sky, forty degrees in January. It was also something they had achieved together: reality.

Now they were imagining in words together. Arlette invented the story and Doek wrote it down. Arlette applied the colour and Doek gave it 'body'. He was the body and she the soul.

Was she really doing this? Did she really drive their car to the station, giving up, making an end of it, stopping? With her diaries in all the colours of the rainbow and the twenty Patrick O'Brians? The fountain pen? Is this what she was? Was this her life? Was this her story?

Did she see it correctly or was it Doek's vision, Doek's greys and moreover Doek's black and white? Some modern film directors used black and white deliberately. In photography too, black and white was chic. Was it sincere or for the effect? Doek had done the colour test, and he had failed. And she? As far as she remembered, she had never been tested: for colours or whatever. Yes, of course, her eyes had been tested when she needed glasses because of her age.

She could always turn around at the station and undo what could be undone. Train, bus and tram lines didn't have colours; they had letters and numbers. Travelling by public transport did not mean nailing your colours to the mast. She could go back. Or was that nailing your colours to the mast after all? A primary colour? Blue? Or something Anglo-Saxon in between everything like peach pink, apple red, lemon yellow. Doek wouldn't do that as it wasn't Dutch, the in-between colours. He had a thing about colours and culture.

'Look at this.'

Doek held up a card of their bird game *Wingspan*. He kept the card in the palm of his raised hand so that only someone standing behind him,

Arlette, could see the picture. A secret sign. Just like the uncle in the post office of Gdansk in Volkert Schlöndorff's *Die Blechtrommel*, Arlette thought. Oh Doek.

'The blue of the kingfisher, now that's what I call blue. Or should I call it azure? I thought that azure was darker. The Italian soccer team, they are called the Azzurri, the deep blue. That blue is almost "navy blue". See: blue is not blue.'

Doek was going deeper than deep: a kind of primary deep.

'And blue here in August, is not like blue in say Kalamaki. 'Cause our August is spring.'

The inaccuracy of colours. You don't see what you see. Words don't mean what you think. Maybe they say: we love each other. Oh Doek.

46

Max Beckmann

Rowena Lennox

Did your mother die, Max Beckmann?
Did she leave a stained-glass
window of blue sails in her house?
Did she go in the water
and never really come out?

Did you lose
the way she arranged
the crockery in her cupboards
before you were ready to?

What did you do then?
What shapes and colours
did you make?
Did you paint thick black outlines
to keep the whole world
from dissolving?
Did those outlines keep you
from drifting
out to sea?

Did those colours bleed, Max Beckmann?
When those discrete compartments
that separate
colour from colour
shape from shape

blood from water
cerebellum from brainstem
no longer held,
did her blood try to find the water
like a river flowing to the sea?

47

The Blue Alice

on seeing Charles Blackman's paintings exhibited in a hospital hallway

Ronald Atilano

I can see Blackman stealing
into the premises last night,
a tuxedoed rabbit
changing the paintings
in the Neurology hallway

for this morning's little girl
who cranes her neck
as they wheel her past
goth-eyed Alice,
the sleepless tea party

of chessboards, misplaced
shoes, falling flowers.
She wakes into a blue dream,
curiouser and curiouser,
on her way to the MRI.

48

Prayer Bones

Rozanna Lilley

Grace was on her knees, cleaning the linoleum floor, a grid pattern of fawn and beige rectangles gradually revealed by the morning sun skidding through the kitchen window, wedged open to catch the sea breeze. The hiss of sprinklers on summer lawns merged with the bristled staccato of her scrubbing—a suburban medley. Another Sunday morning in Bridgewater.

As she rose, spider-veined legs gradually unfolding, Grace admired her handiwork. She muttered, 'Let all things be done decently and in order,' a half-smile playing across her lips, uncertain of the propriety of fully forming. Her domestic reverie was interrupted by the smack of flesh hitting the concrete pavement, a child's cry ricocheting the cul-de-sac.

Changing into a freshly ironed A-line skirt and a floral-patterned polyester blouse, Grace crossed the narrow hallway, knocking on her son's bedroom door. If he was quick, he could still make it to church. It was her third attempt to raise him from the dead. The knock became a rap, followed by a guttural groan.

'Leave me alone.' Luke protested.

'Are you sure you won't come into town with me? The service should be lovely today.'

Christmas had always been her favourite time of year. An artificial tree took pride of place in the lounge, weighed down by fairy lights and hand-made decorations—spiral snowmen and paper snowflakes testament to the passing years. A gauzy winged angel was speared to the plastic crown.

Silence. She opened the door a crack, pushing against a pile of discarded clothes. She could just make out a doona-wrapped lump on one side of the bed, a skewwhiff poster of a unicorn prancing in front of a rainbow framing his inertia. Once it had been his older sister's room. Luke pulled a pillow over his head.

Grace retreated, throwing the house keys into her bulging purse. The clasp squeezed shut as she hurried down the serpentine path, passing the sepia clumps of buffalo grass that fringed the modest patch of yard. When they had first moved in, she could hardly believe her luck. Almost two years on the waiting list and finally a place she could call her own, somewhere the kids could thrive. And, to top it all off, a built-in robe, tiered shelving like a promise of prosperity.

Opening the galvanised gate, she brushed against the single rose bush, planted the week they arrived, a spade borrowed from two doors down, a handful of fertiliser tossed in. Her blouse snagged on a Cinderella thorn, a single drop of blood pooling in the scratch. Grace dashed for the bus.

The trip to town took almost an hour. All the other passengers were head-deep in their phones. At Bridgewater Plaza, an elderly couple hailed the bus. Leaning on a walker, the wife was all mauve hair and steely determination. That'll be me in ten years, Grace thought. The two of them took forever to board, shuffling towards the accessible seats. At this rate, she would be late for the 10 a.m. service.

Contemplating the receding line of fast-food outlets, Grace pulled out a biro and a book of quick crosswords from her cardigan pocket, a gift from Luke last Christmas. He'd bought it at the local newsagent along with a hot firemen calendar. She couldn't bring herself to hang it on the wall. What if she had a visitor? She stashed it in the built-in robe, along with all the other accumulated crap.

The clue for seven down read: '164-foot-tall movie star'. She thought of Fay Wray in a gossamer gown struggling to escape her fate, the black and white TV screen flickering. But King Kong didn't fit. She clicked her retractable biro up and down as she thought. Of course, Godzilla! All those years of watching Luke on his PlayStation had finally paid off. Until he took up burnouts and bongs, she hadn't realised it would be possible to feel nostalgic about monsters with beam attacks, the steady simplicity of a victorious roar.

From the interchange, Grace hurried through the city, admiring the neatly trimmed pines festooned with floppy faux velvet bows, towards the old hall. In her parents' day, it had been a popular ballroom. After a few sherries, her mother loved to tell the story of how she had first met her future husband doing the Madison, locking eyes somewhere between Two Up and Two Back and Cuddle Me. When the recollection was trotted out, year after year, Grace had always feigned surprise.

At the entrance, she gave the push bar on the double doors a decisive shove. On the other side, an usher shook her hand, a beatific smile plastered across his pimpled face, pointing to a seat towards the back of the neatly formed rows of collapsible chairs. Some of the congregants turned. She flushed, a startling shade of puce spreading from her neck to her cheeks.

A handful of young people took their places on the raised wooden platform, adjusting their double denim and strumming their guitars. The tinny tune made Grace think of the music box with a spinning ballerina that once took pride of place on her dressing table, stiff lilac tutu turning to the strains of *Sleeping Beauty*. At fifty-nine, she had stopped hoping for a handsome prince. As she well knew, life was no fairy tale.

Pastor Ted entered from the wings, an audible ripple reverberating around the hall. His thinning hair was vigorously parted to one side; a chunky Rolex knock-off circled his meaty wrist; peeking above loafers his left sock joked *Jesus walks*, his right sock *Ted talks*. On cue, Grace stood and clapped, arms upraised to receive the Holy Spirit.

'Let us turn from our sins and turn towards the mercy of Jesus', the sermon began. 'God sent forth the perfect gift, his son, born on Christmas Day. We all know the story of the three wise men, of the gifts they brought to celebrate His birth—"When they had opened their treasures, they presented unto him gifts: gold, and frankincense, and myrrh." But do you know what those gifts mean?'

Pastor Ted quizzically surveyed his congregation, a brusque motion indicating they should sit.

'Maybe some of you are hoping for particular gifts this Christmas. Maybe you covet a new pair of runners, or you think your diet might work if you just had a portable smoothie maker.'

An appreciative laugh circulated the hall, a stout woman towards the front adding 'Amen'.

'Maybe you are thinking about your kids,' Pastor Ted continued. 'Perhaps they would like a new bike or a fancy skateboard. The wise men who came from the East did some Christmas shopping too. Each of their gifts had a specific meaning—gold for His kingship on earth; frankincense, a symbol of His divinity; and myrrh, an ointment used to prepare bodies for burial, a sign of His future suffering.'

He looked up from his pulpit.

'Yes, sometimes the Bible is grim.' To alleviate the sombre mood, he offered a casual aside: 'By the way, I don't recommend you give any of these gifts to your kids.'

The audience tittered.

'But I do recommend that you think about what it is that we are really celebrating. The gift that God gave us at Christmas is a Saviour. And the same Spirit that anointed Jesus has been poured into our hearts, right here and right now.' The congregation rose for a second time, a zealous chorus of 'Praise God' repeating in syncopated waves.

When Pastor Ted instructed his flock to hit their prayer bones, Grace gratefully fell to the floor. At first, she thought about her children. It was easy to pray for Luke—there was so much he didn't have: a job, a girlfriend, some ambition. But it was difficult to know where to start with Ella. It had been so long since she'd seen her daughter that it was getting hard to even bring her face firmly to mind. Grace felt a little dizzy. Maybe it was because she had hurried from the interchange or maybe it was because she found it hard to forgive Ella, the way she'd just up and left for the Mainland, making accusatory remarks about how her mother had joined the ranks of the happy-clappy as she hauled her suitcase out the door. It was a dry-eyed goodbye. And then, radio silence.

The booming of Pastor Ted's voice pulled her back inside the hall. He asked if anyone knew the time. A young man consulted his Fitbit, calling out '11 am!'

'The hands of the Doomsday Clock are moving ever closer to midnight,' replied Pastor Ted. 'The world is perilously close to the precipice.'

He listed the scourge of pandemics, the threat of nuclear annihilation, increasing floods and famine as indisputable evidence that the Devil walks amongst us. Squeezing her eyes shut, Grace summoned an image of Satan wading through Victoria Dock, effortlessly crushing yachts and motor cruises with his scaly claws, his fiery breath unleashing destruction across the city, the corner tower of the GPO crumbling to dust beneath his cloven hooves.

Pastor Ted's words began to spin and shift in front of her, a dazzling kaleidoscope. As the colours of his apocalyptic tirade fragmented, Grace found herself drifting in a calm current, surrounded by an ocean of blue: electric indigo, periwinkle, sapphire. If only she could stay floating in that bejewelled landscape forever.

When Grace made landfall, she joined the congregation in singing *The Comforter has Come*. Following the hymn, Pastor Ted placed their sins before Jesus, asking that the Holy Spirit wash them away with the blood of the lamb. A final song of praise and it was all over for another week.

Grace picked up her purse. Her skirt was creased where she had knelt; she tried to smooth it down but it remained obstinately crumpled. In the street, the harsh glare of daylight and the clamour of traffic seemed unreal. She felt as though she was stretched, pulled towards a space opening up deep inside her.

God moves in mysterious ways, she thought.

At the butchers, she admired the nativity scene in the window, Baby Jesus flanked by slabs of steak sunbaking on artificial grass, and queued for a leg of lamb. Sunday night roast was a non-negotiable. Triumphantly clutching her shopping, she boarded the bus. There was still laundry to wash, potatoes to peel, rubbish to put out. If there was time, she could watch *Antique Roadshow*—there was something so soothing about all those collectibles, their owners jostling for attention, on the verdant lawns of manor houses. Approaching the bridge, ragged clouds were reflected in the Derwent, a turquoise ribbon unspooling towards Storm Bay. Grace wriggled, a damp sensation spreading across her lap. When she looked down, she saw that the blood of the lamb had leached through the brown paper bag, her crumpled skirt stained a sticky dark brick red.

49

Der Blaue Berg

Mike Ladd

Kandinsky escaped Stalin,
lived quietly as an old man
under the Nazis in Paris—
survived just long enough
to see the city liberated.

His horse riders
on the Blue Mountain
are joy itself.
The colours galloping,
the riders joined but free—
charging uphill
into ultramarine hinterland:
hope
before the apocalypse.

50

Building, Antenna, Span & Earth

Isabella G Mead

In the interview, the BASE jumper admits
a tense relationship with his mother.
On waking each flinched morning,
she prepares for the blow—malfunction, mis-
calculation, the fact of the ground.
The constancy of unrealised grief
sours her tongue, turns her speech brittle
& against him. I am thinking of the BASE
jumper's mother as our daughter sleeps
in thick water between us. On the question
of adult children, you declare unconditional
support for any future passion, including
BASE jumping. I see the sky emptied
of cloud, emboldened in blue, & the field
blazing green, silent but for the keen whistle
of a footloose wind. In this terrible place,
my heart rebels against your casual belief
that *everything will be okay*, even as the hospital
looms—a white mountain. On the fourth floor,
the doctor confirms the baby must out.
I draw my hands to the hard bubble
of my want, feel her shimmy in response.
Labour progresses until it stalls spectacularly.
Through an emergency exit carved in skin,
our theoretical BASE jumper emerges, breath-
taking & bathed in fluorescent light. Reverent,
you hold her as if she is not flesh & blood
but gold & glass. Looking into her eyes—alert,

dark blue with knowledge—you weep. I fall
into place. She is mine & not mine, her hair
an unexpected shade of yellow. In the aftermath,
we soften our stances, find a common span.
This is how incaution prevails, worries disperse—
in faulty wingsuit, the future disappears,
swallowed whole in the pink mouth of the present,
that vast open space, our daughter's new life.

51

The Blue Man

Julie Egan

Eleanor first saw him silhouetted against the glare of a bright hot summer morning. She was in the laundry pushing the sheets down into the soapy water when she heard the doorbell. She paused. The other housemaid, Lily, usually answered the door. The bell rang again, and she laid down the stick and dried her soapy arms and pulled down her sleeves. When she opened the door, she saw two men. Miners. The younger man held his left wrist in his right hand and winced every time he breathed.

'Is the doctor in?' asked the older man. 'I think he's broken something.'

'The doctor's out. But he'll be back for lunch. You can wait out the back.'

She was about to direct them around to the back of the house when they stepped through the door into the dim cool hall. Their feet crunched on the polished floor. She led them through the house to a bench against the wall outside the doctor's surgery.

'Do you think we could have some water?' asked the older man.

His face looked as though a rain cloud had settled on it. When she handed him the water, she noticed that his hands were a soft grey-blue.

'Silver,' he said, noticing her glance. 'I'm full of silver. From the mines. Llywernog mine. Lead and silver.'

'I'm Welsh too,' she said. 'My father was a miner. Coal.'

'So, he would have been black,' the blue man laughed.

She remembered her father coming home black with coal dust and her mother boiling up water every afternoon to fill the tin bath placed before the fire.

She heard footsteps from inside the house. 'That must be the doctor. I'll tell him you're here.'

On her way back to the laundry she met Lily coming down the stairs.

'You should see the man outside. His skin, it's blue.' said Eleanor.

'Haven't you seen him before?' said Lily. 'He's Welsh, come out here to try his luck with the gold. Used to be a silver miner. They get that sometimes, breathing the silver in all the time. The doctor says there's a name for it. Should be in a sideshow.'

She was hanging the heavy wet sheets on the line when she saw him later that day. He stood on the other side of the fence in the shade, his hat pulled down over his brow.

'I received a parcel from home with a newspaper. I thought you'd like to read it. Old news now.' He held it out to her.

She looked back to the house and down to the basket of washing. 'My hands are wet.'

'I'll leave it in the kitchen, shall I?' he said.

She longed to reach out and rub her wet finger against his skin. She imagined the blue-grey coming off on her finger and leaving a white patch behind.

After that she often saw him in town. Unlike the other miners who spent their days above ground sprawling in the sun, he hugged the shadows, sitting in the cool of a verandah or under a tree.

'Don't you enjoy the sun?' she said.

'I love it,' he said, 'but this gets worse if I'm in the sun too much.' He pointed to his skin. 'That's why mining suits me.' She liked the way he carried his history on his face. Like her, she thought. She sought the shadows too. Her scar snaked through one eyebrow, across her nose and down her cheek. That and seven years transportation had been the legacy of the fight.

'You're a bit like me,' she said. 'Everyone has a story, but people can see our stories.'

Sometimes he'd bring newspapers for her to read. 'If you're ever homesick you should talk to me,' he said. 'Touch me. I've got a little bit of Wales in me. Genuine Welsh silver. You could mine me.'

'I have a favour to ask,' he said one day. 'Will you come and have your portrait taken with me?'

'Why?'

'My mother. She wants to know what I look like now.' He shuffled his feet. 'And I lied, I told her I was married. She wants to see my wife.'

'You should have chosen someone prettier.'

Mr Anderson at Anderson's Photographic Portrait Establishment positioned Eleanor carefully so that her profile showed as little as possible of her scar. 'Just look at your young man,' he said.

They held hands.

'This is what they use the silver for,' the blue man said. 'Making photographs. I'm a walking photograph.'

'But you're bluish, not black and white.'

'Must be the blood in the skin,' he said, 'changes the colour.'

'It wouldn't be such a bad thing,' he said.

'What?'

'Us getting married.'

The wedding was held in the late afternoon to avoid the heat and glare of the day. They danced in the deep blue night under the moon. His fingers traced the line of her scar and when she kissed him, she imagined she could feel tiny grains of silver in his lips.

52

Driving Discomfort

Jake Dennis

Sunday on our new route home
a hearse, polished as patent leather,
enters our journey. It has rained
and the rain has fallen off the jarrah
onto this river of asphalt. Sunlight drips

through the canopy. Always guided
by signs, we rush within the law
to overtake the hearse beside us,
solid and cool as onyx
carrying twin baby-blue coffins.

In tropical climes, if you are blessed,
you notice behind you,
Papilio memnon agenor
on a leaf or flower, or someone else's
windowsill. My lover grabs

my hand and we pray as our tyres rip
the river. *Not today, but when, Lord, let us*
stay together. May we rest in one boat
of flowers and flames, not shovelled
in dark like those pursuing two

soon-swallowed blue pills. We look back
as we speed away, change lanes
like organ recipients. *Lord, let us stay.*
My hand on her thigh, in the mirror:
the hearse and brown eyes. On both sides

of this road, beneath the forests
are caves still drinking the rain. Darling,
will it be you or me? Some day
only one of us will learn, your lover
almost always goes first.

53

Bluejohn

Anna McHugh

Every age has its chemical crutch. Prozac, Oxycontin, Xanax, Ritalin, Viagra—they reflect our struggle to meet the demands of a merciless world.

After the long months of lockdown, feeding on the slush pile of memories in all forms, we had become unbearable to ourselves. Entrepreneurs being what they are, a product was invented to solve the problem. Bluejohn, also known as JS, Johnsmith, and Blur, made bearable the return to the ceaseless tyranny by wiping out the stockpile of yesterdays which caused so much grief.

Originally designed by Doxis Pharma under the name Librimeme, the drug was a PKMζ inhibitor prescribed to veterans, asylum-seekers, and domestic abuse victims whose trauma-addled hippocampi could no longer cope with long-term memory. (The hippocampus files and planes short-term memories into some kind of shape, then sends them off to the unknown realms of long-term memory).

Librimeme provided a brief respite from the task of making new long-term memories. Most pleasing to the FDA, Librimeme left short-term memory unimpaired, which meant that you could still be expected to hold down a job while you dealt with memories of your legs being blown off.

Tweaked by business-minded chemists in ethics-free kitchens, the compound received a new name because it induced the peaceful feeling of staring off into the blue mid-distance, happily accepting the gap between you and the subject you can never reach. Bluejohn was a more potent version of Librimeme. It released you from the memory of stressful events, which meant that you were largely released from the impact of life.

Once you embarked on Bluejohn, you were like the dead in Dante's *Divine Comedy*, liberated from the (neural) bodies with which you made new memories. While Librimeme had been intended for extremely short-term use under strict supervision, Bluejohn had a devoted long-term following. Graduates began to take it when they entered the workforce, to cope with the fact that two-thirds of their lives were unconscious or unbearable. Mothers began to take it after giving birth: you could remember the joys of pregnancy without the horrors of postnatal blues, the inevitable quarrelling, the lonely disintegration of self in the face of a child's rapacity for all your time and energy. Those orphaned or retrenched by the pandemic took it to prevent themselves realising the extent of their situation.

Upon starting Bluejohn, the world shrank to a space around four hours long. After that, everything was new again. Biographical, implicit, and procedural memory was entirely intact. Memories from before Bluejohn were intact: you still knew that you were Bill Tucker, who was a left-hander with a good golf-swing, a dentist, and who drove a vintage Falcon. But your wife's affair, discovered the previous week, or your despair at the prospect of more days staring at porous molars, and the exhaustion which caused you to look longingly at your own handgun, was gone, wiped clean like a kitchen surface in a commercial.

Addicted to this gentle amnesia, people found they could bear not only each other, but themselves. It was possible to enjoy each day when you could remember being a teenager, and events after lunch, but nothing in between. Like a gambler walking away from the tables, the trick was to judge when you'd accrued enough good long-term memories and were on the inevitable turn to the bad. Then Bluejohn entered, not legally but not entirely illegally either. Arguments, stressors, disappointments and exhaustion were experienced for a maximum of four hours then neatly binned.

Use of Post-it notes and electronic reminders surged, but the decline of health-, life- and income-insurance conclusively proved that fear of the future derived largely from memories of the past.

Since it was an American product, other countries soon became dismayed about, and then reactive towards, the influx of American amnesia. To promote their own brand—variously named *Azul*, *Principe Azul*, and *Siniye*—they applied tariffs in the name of curbing the Bluejohn Crisis. With cheaper domestic products, use went up even more until entire nations had forgotten each other and lived, like contented babies, in a placid and eternal present.

54

Treatise on the Cyanometer

Autumn Royal and Hana Pera Aoake

No. 1

This comprises bodies and souls—entwined—never separate. With significant unity, we suppose the body/soul is blue. If I describe my body/soul to you—feel how lyrical formations are expressed through the mouth, echoing the atmosphere you are composed of and, as such, resembling the external colours of the organs, earth, water, and sky.

No. 2

We contend that the body/soul is more than a statue or earthen machine—some higher power has willed the formation of what is entirely possible and impossible. Interrogation is the formation of the premise, and universality is imagined as blue since this is how this earth is photographed from space.

No. 3

Blue may be a time marker, but it is never quantifiable. The Genevan geologist, meteorologist, physicist, and mountaineer Horace Bénédict de Saussure spent much of his life trying to understand his external surroundings—creating a cyanometer to measure the colour *blue*. He has been documented as the first person to build a solar-powered oven and, as a scientist, sought to categorise the phenomenal world—the apparent reason we have alpinism and meteorology. Such sky-blue classifications inspire us to create a DIY cyanometer for our project of the week. It is vital to have a project—no matter the air pollution.

No. 4

Love is not fixed, and accidents are expensive. Think about this and the obsidian teeth in between Hine-nui-te-pō's vagina and imagine a blue-black tongue like one of Freud's Chow Chows. That old man tried to play four—knick-knack-paddy-whacking bones against the door. Pledge to error, error, error until you discover the entire truth of blue.

No. 5

Everyone talks about the infinite blueness of the Mediterranean Sea. I thought it was dirty. More brown than blue. I swallow the waves to reciprocate this relationship.

No. 6

Her body/soul drove the blue car, with a ducktail spoiler, into the air and across the highway border. If she were still alive, she would ask my mother behind the counter at the café for a berry smoothie on her lunch break. If she were awake, I would call her, no matter the hour—I trust she would recognise my voice.

No. 7

We object to drinking from Spode's *steccato* teacup, with its arresting stripes in rich cobalt blue and contrasting lines decorating the saucer's rim. You have not lost control of the game, but you also cannot hold it while creating banal partitions with an index finger. Sink into the splendour that will always be mediocre before the terror of being created drifts into collapsible horizons.

No. 8

I feel unnatural when gazing at the ocean, not because of literary-historical descriptions of the *wine-dark sea*—but because of listening to the stories of the land I have occupied since my ancestors settled. Regardless of this knowledge, the relationship does not change, nor does the perspective or longing for connection—nothing is never without consequence.

No. 9

During the seminar on the psychogeography of grief, we sat together in blue, absorbing how proximity and subject dictate a spectrum of difficulty regarding expression. Mimesis of language is impossible in this instance, and my neurological symptoms have returned—are returning. My left eye droops—I initially wrote *sags*, but *droops* may convey the physicality of the eyes despite Maurice Merleau-Ponty's claim that *words do not look like the things they designate.*

No. 10

There are many words for blue in te reo Māori. When a word like *kikorangi* or *kahurangi* appears, you think about the rangi part of the word referring to Ranginui—the sky father, who longs to be reunited with his lover Papatūānuku—earth mother.

No. 11

While it is not banal, a sink filled with magnificent desire is often dismissed, and stagnancy can madden you if you are too alert to its existence. In error, I googled *tristesse* instead of *treatise* and was informed that *tristesse* is a French word that means sadness. My body/soul also absorbs that post-coital *tristesse* is defined as a feeling of melancholy, unease, distress, or hostility after orgasm.

No. 12

I dance slowly to get it *sexxxy* by *red sexxxy under* a blue light with a blue Bic in hand.

No. 13

My veins protrude, and past attempts at escape humble me—I feel the sun on my weak and tired wrists and remember veins are bluish-green because of how the light reacts to skin and blood. Blue blood, blue collar, what is the distinction—lightly dramatic?

No. 14

Overnight, we soak the blackberries to bring out all the worms and other bugs, then freeze them, before making a pie—the inside of the pastry turns blue-black like a Chow Chow's tongue. We will consume this as a dessert.

No. 15

I/you take a turn into the deep blue. So profoundly and so blue into the absence of certainty—the place we imagine when thinking about death and its beyond—the end of toxicity.

No. 16

My facial paralysis has taken hold, and I have again lost my ability to smile, assuming the way I curved my mouth was perceived as *smiling*. When it is time to stand, my left leg drags my desire to raise my head toward the ceiling—the one beneath the sky—no longer visibly blue—and this all feels derivative. I would not wish for my body to be written about by anyone but me.

No. 17

A friend messaged me about Derek Jarman. I first saw Jarman's *Blue* by chance in Barcelona. Afterwards, I saw everything with a blue filter. *O blue come forth, O blue arise, O blue ascend, O blue come in.*

No. 18

The sky is always blue other than when the Burdekin Dam bursts with grey-coloured blue skies, that perfect blue *kikorangi* (as we would say in te reo Māori) ominously shines through in the middle of the storm—before the wind picks up and shakes everything around you with reckless abandon—poetic with static electricity.

No. 19

Lighting erupts purple into the night sky—and seeing the books my ex-lovers read on Goodreads fills me with baby-blue satisfaction. There is a comment that while one of my recently published books has been *nominated for some award* [sic] *it was ok* [sic] *but not one* [sic] *that really stimulated me* [sic], *some good ideas though.* I think about the word *stimulation*, and I am thankful my labour did not arouse anything within this man—so my blue-light wavelengths may belong to others [sic].

No. 20

I lay down on the paper sheets, my head tilted to the left, and listened to the wheels on the road, realising there were some acts beyond ideology, but I cannot yet name them. All I know is that this is not an end or a death but a foundational point for the blue and disheartened to be judged by what we think of as glorification.

No. 21

The blue paint in the house I am renting has been muted with white. (Mix cobalt blue with titanium white to achieve the Mr Frosty tone by Dulux—*helping Australians change their homes and communities since 1918*). This explanation still does not allow me to summarise how this muted blue was created and why it is disturbing. Perhaps it is a body floating above the river when there is no spell for revival—a gap to fall through. This is not a spell or an equation for knowledge—the expectation of the lyrical *I/eye* is coated too deeply into the colour itself—floating in doubtful frost.

No. 22

I swim in Tarawera's tears.

No. 23

This striptease is essential for anyone keen on a relevant and pragmatic grasp of the progressive wisdom we are surveying. Clergy, students, sceptics, scholars, and people in pews will find this wisdom thoroughly informative and profoundly illuminating—blue. It is immensely intellectual and accessible, much like the clothes you wear while reading this. I enjoy leading, yet I find writing reports tedious.

No. 24

The *Pale Blue Dot* is a photograph of Earth taken on Valentine's Day in 1990. It's taken from the Voyager 1 space probe from approximately six billion kilometres away.

No. 25

There are two colours I associate with you—blue and red. I wore brilliant blue earrings made by a Cree woman and a wrap-around vintage Miss Crabb that is Chartreuse and silk with wine and oil stains on it. I think of the dress I wore—my Vivien Leigh as Scarlett O'Hara dress—to the art fair and think about how we were all in a fish tank encircled by grey-blue cunning sharks stalking us, and now my daughter is afraid of the ocean because she thinks sharks will eat her and the drone footage shows sharks encircling us slowly—but it is their home not ours. Vivien Leigh approached the director of *Gone with the Wind* dressed out of context for her audition as Scarlett O'Hara—she got the part. Leigh's eyes have been recorded as grey but sometimes blue. The truth—is *Gone with the Wind* the first film produced in colour?

No. 26

Feeling your skin welt in the sun always makes you think of a school camp you reluctantly went to on at a cattle station in North Queensland where you slept in old railway cattle cables with dark blue sheets that smelt like raw lamb chops and as an activity—we children aged 12-13, took turns branding a cow. I could not do it, but the most god-awful boys in your class relished the opportunity to hurt an animal existing only as food and walked around drenched in red dirt—drinking dirty water.

No. 27

If I could measure blue—I think of the calmness of wanting. I want to feel the way that I feel that I should feel—so proud about it. I want to explain why I am not *beyond blue*, even if the *baby blues* have long passed. But the history of your presence never comes into it, it is all about your future and the paradox is—you must end something present before it starts—as in hanging up the phone.

No. 28

The colour blue has been said to encompass all of time's emotion and non-linearity squeezed into each memory—but not a dotted line that is sequential as you imagine moving on the page, even though I have cracked swimming pools and sand-pit shapes like a sapphire seashell, and dried blue clay, and the one-paraumu whose volcanic origin glints blue. It is the same soil Kupe cupped in his hand. All this teleporting between time exists in flashes because your daughter's eyes were blue for a year, then they turned green, and now they seem to be shifting into being hazel.

No. 29

During the first night in our new rental, my partner found me asleep with my eyes open. The next night, they sleepwalked over the navy-blue couch I bought from Fantastic Furniture. I was troubled by the idea of feet on the couch in this way, like I am about people who wear shoes inside, but I am more disturbed that they are a person who can fall asleep anywhere. It reminded me of the trouble I have always had with falling asleep in the first place. Often, I close my eyes and see flits of blue squares, which I know now to be called *phosphenes*. They occur when there is pressure on the eyeball's interior, causing the nerves in the retina to convulse and fire up. Our brain does not know the difference between that and an actual image, so it interprets this as just flashes of colour.

No. 30

I think about my mother's and sister's eyes—both blue. I have spent all my money (via instalments on Afterpay) to procure a pair of earrings so their eye colour dangles off my ears. I have only worn the earrings once to a literati dinner (grazing my right ear against the stucco wall due to my imbalance, thankfully not damaging the jewels). I now keep them in a drawer and look at them occasionally—like a Sally Rooney novel.

No. 31

Something for pleasure rather than gain—but I am not swearing. Once, I had a metallic blue bikini a dancer named Bambi gifted to me. Bambi is a bodybuilder now. She has blue and red hair—without exchange.

No. 32

In *When we cease to understand the world* Benjamin Labatut writes that Cyanide originates from a by-product isolated in 1782 from the first modern synthetic pigment—Prussian blue—by the Swiss pigment maker and dyer, Johann Jacob Diesbach. It happened accidentally while he was trying to create another version of a ruby red colour taken from the blood of the highly fragile cochineals, which were stolen and brought to Europe by Conquistadors after they invaded South America. Diesbach thought he had discovered *hsbd-iryt*—the original colour of the sky. This recipe for blue was passed down over centuries, with the formula stolen by a Greek man that, in time, was lost after the fall of the Roman Empire.

No. 33

You imagine your insides turning blue, stained with blue cordial or the rocket launcher blue lagoon 2L box mixer you once drank alone, leaving a party you stole it from and as if without thinking and in a hazy, temperamental, drunken stupor or blue-bruised love trance, you took to his house. He is with someone else, and you see through the window and run and vomit blue and think of his grandmother saying that she borrowed her mother's pearls, but the blue she had at her wedding was dried blue cornflowers in her bouquet.

No. 34

A blue-collar worker declares bankruptcy in pursuit of upward social mobility—white polyester roses now flourish on a grave.

No. 35

We talk over each other because we get too excited about talking. Love largely stems from the daily routines of sharing a space. I enjoy arguing with you despite also hating it and its lack of resolution—which does not lead to fucking. In *Bluets*, Maggie Nelson devotes space to fucking—she describes intimate moments at the Chelsea Hotel. We were perplexed when she found the time and money, and time and money again for such encounters. There is no fucking here—aside from this reference for the lack of fucking.

No. 36

My nightmares often involve unintentionally killing loved ones in domestic settings or while performing mundane activities. Recently, my foot mistakenly pressed the accelerator instead of the brake, leading us through a red light in Aotearoa at a hazardous intersection you warned me about. These nightmares are connected to my love for someone who killed a parent, whom they still love—in a bed I have also slept in many times. I cannot use the word *murder*, even though the media cherished this flexible word as both noun and verb—but the one that numbs my body/soul is the word *slain*, the past participle of the verb *slay*. Blue is the divider here.

No. 37

It is like being put in knots. I want to win, be right, be funny, be snarky, or be vicious, but I never, ever, not for a second, would stop being in love—*a clear cerulean when new.*

No. 38

Blue is editing an interview with a famous writer claiming her children use specific phrases due to being raised around literate people—mistakenly linking language acquisition with literacy. My semi-illiterate parents have always relied on me to translate their letters, emails, and legal documents, which I owe to them—but I know it diminishes their autonomy.

No. 39

I simply cannot and will not measure the colour blue. I could never get a sense of its form despite 40 stops with 53 degrees. We start at 0 for white and 52 for black. I think a lot about how you cannot create the colour white because it is considered a base colour. A clear, cloudless sky is blue because molecules in the air scatter blue light from the sun more than they scatter red light. When we look towards the sun at sunset—we see red and orange colours because the blue light has been scattered out and away from the line of sight. Out of sight, out of mind.

No. 40

Memories are uncoiling—water pushes all the doors open, and as if an error—my body/soul flops out a blue-black tongue panting for the deluge.

Coda

The Sound Blue Makes

Blue is a liminal space.
It is that which haunts.
The ghost that hovers between life and death, between yes and no.
It is the boundary: *I have given enough.*
How do we go forward? How do we go back?
How do we stay in the present moment when it won't stop echoing?

Blue is the taste of regret, and the promise of hope.
The ache of writing—and waiting.
Breath held, underwater,
for someone, somewhere, to praise it. To publish it. To make it matter.
It is the grief and fury of AI reshaping our worlds, our words, our bodies.
The blue of oceans rising—and the drowning we pretend not to see.

These are not soft cries on bathroom tiles. These are war cries.
Data that exposes. That unravels.
The mask drops. We are bleeding.
Nostalgia so bitter it splits memory. Is memory fact, or fiction?

Blue is not just a lament.
It is a rebirth.
A reckoning.
The song we sing over ourselves when we mourn—but also, when we rise.

But this collection is not a dirge. It is a resurrection.
It is the sound blue makes when it refuses to be quiet.
It is memory with blood in its mouth, and hope like a blade between its teeth.

We chose these works not because they matched the brief,
but because they made us feel—like we were falling, gasping,
coming back to life.

Adara Rose Luis, Co-Editor

About the Contributors

Geoffrey Aitken writes on Adelaide's unceded Kaurna land and is an award-winning minimalist poet leaning into his 'lived experience disability' for publishers in multiple countries worldwide. Recent works have been published in *Verge 2024: Click* (AUS) & *ZiN Daily* (HR), and a forthcoming piece will appear in *The Engine(idling* (US). Geoffrey was nominated for publication in the *Best of the Net* anthology in 2022.

Anonymous is a postgraduate student at Monash University, studying literature and sociology, hoping to work somewhere in the publishing industry. They are passionate about experimental/hybrid contemporary texts and emerging genreless fiction, poetry and short stories. They like to read things that make them question everything.

Hana Pera Aoake (Ngāti Mahuta, Ngāti Hinerangi, Tainui/Waikato) is an artist and writer from Aotearoa. In 2020, they published *A Bathful of Kawakawa and Hot Water* (Compound Press). In 2025 they published 'Blame it on the rain' (no more poetry) and *Some Helpful Models of Grief* (Compound Press).

Jude Aquilina's poetry, stories and articles are published across Australia and abroad. She is the author of several poetry collections, including *Knifing the Ice* and *On a Moon Spiced Night* (Wakefield Press). Jude teaches creative writing and is a member of International PEN and Asia Pacific Writers and Translators.

Ronald Araña Atilano is a Filipino-born poet who lives in Awabakal land in Lake Macquarie, New South Wales. His works have been published in the *Rabbit Poetry Journal*, *Westerly Magazine*, *Jacaranda Journal UQ*, the Booranga Writers' Centre's *fourW* anthology and Spineless Wonders' *Remnants* Microlit anthology. His poem 'The Fugitive' was highly commended in the 2023 Hammond House International Literary Prize.

Tara Bazargan lives in Melbourne/Naarm, where she studies medicine and literature at Monash University. Her poetry is her attempt at making sense of the world, and has been extensively published in her Notes app.

John Bennett hitchhiked to Australia and stayed. He is a widely published poet, has won major Australian prizes, published four books and taught ecological literature. He is heavily involved in the cultural life of northern NSW and reads poems live on ABC Regional radio once a week.

Maria Bonar's writing has appeared in *Award Winning Australian Writing, Green Ink Poetry, Catchment: Poetry of Place, Poetry d'Amour, Rochford Street Review, Bronze Quill Winners Anthology, Stringybark Stories, BootsnAll,* and numerous anthologies and online publications. She won the 2024 Creatrix Poetry Prize. She lives in Perth, Western Australia.

Richard Calam is a retired educator and writer. He has had extensive experience in curriculum writing and worked as a speechwriter and researcher for the Ohio Arts Council.

Gayelene Carbis's second poetry collection, *I Have Decided to Remain Vertical* (Puncher and Wattmann), won the Eyelands Writer's Choice Award 2025 (Greece) and the Eyelands Poetry Book Award 2024. She was also recently Finalist/Highly Commended/Distinguished Favourite in poetry book awards in the UK and the US, and in the NSW Society of Women Writers' Poetry Book Award. Gayelene writes poetry, prose, short films and plays.

Megan Cartwright is an Australian poet and college Literature teacher. Her credits include *Barrelhouse Magazine*, *Contemporary Verse 2*, *Cordite Poetry Review* and *Island Magazine*. She is the winner of the 2025 Tina Kane Emergent Writer Award.

Musician and writer **Sofia Chapman** is a professional accordionist with the band Vardos. Sofia has presented many plays at Midsumma Festival of Queer Arts at La Mama Theatre and has won awards in playwriting, music and bilingual filmmaking. Sofia's poetry was shortlisted for the 2022 Dorothy Porter Poetry Prize.

Afifa Kamal Chaudhry is a writer from Lahore. Her work has been long-listed for the Commonwealth Short Story Prize and the Zeenat Haroon Rashid Writing Prize for Women.

Bill Collopy has had two books published: one novel, *House of Given*, and one textbook on language, *Conquering Beastly Writing*. He has also had stories published in *Overland*, *The Age*, *Dublin Quarterly*, *Sleepers Almanac*, *LinQ*, *Going Down Swinging* and *New England Review*, as well as articles in *Sydney Morning Herald*, *The Age* and *The Australian*.

Lisa Collyer is the author of the poetry collection *How To Order Eggs Sunny Side Up* (shortlisted for The Dorothy Hewett Award), published with Life Before Man. She recently won an artist residence at Bundanon Art Museum, where she will create work on climate grief.

Lucy Connelly is a writer, artist and swimming teacher who currently resides on Bunurong land. She studies Secondary Education and Arts at Monash University. She writes about living with mental illness and grief in hopes of reaching people with similar experiences.

Burmese-Australian Boorloo-based entertainer (singer/poet/actor) **Jake Dennis** @PoetOfJazz had poetry published in over twenty-five publications across twelve countries in 2024. JD is a 2024–2025 Writing WA Emerging Writers Program awardee who won the Open Your Mind and #30in30 Poetry Prizes. QPoetry chapbooks: *The Exhibition* and *Gone*. https://www.PoetOfJazz.com/

Elena Disilvestro is a Venezuelan-Australian writer. Previously published in the 2023 and 2024 editions of *Verge*, she writes fantasy horror stories that resonate with various aspects of her life.

Jane Downing's stories have been published around Australia and overseas, including in *Griffith Review*, *Big Issue*, *Antipodes*, *Westerly*, *Island*, *Overland* and previously in *Verge*. Her novel, *The Sultan's Daughter*, was released by Obiter Publishing in 2020. She can be found at janedowning.wordpress.com

Julie Egan has worked as research virologist, diagnostic microbiologist, science teacher, academic journal editor and museum curator. She is now a freelance science writer and editor based in Melbourne and sometimes writes fiction.

Steve Evans is a prize-winning writer and editor of twenty-three books, including ten of his own poetry. The most recent collection is *The Crow on the Cross* (2024). He was previously Head of English at Flinders University, where he also ran the Creative Writing Program.

Leone Gabrielle writes in the company of crested pigeons and exhausted teacups, from an old hillside house, on Taungurung Country. Shortlisted: Minds Shine Bright, Spineless Wonders, *La Piccioletta Barca*. Published: *Plumwood Mountain*, *Meanjin*, *Rochford St. Review*, *KalliopeX*, *Meniscus*. Debut chapbook, a collaboration with Lucy Wilks: *L+L Exquisite Corpse Sonnets*.

Aries M. Gacutan works on the traditional lands of the Woiwurrung and Boonwurrung peoples of the Kulin Nation, writing poetry about space and place. In 2024, they were awarded the Red Room Emerging Poets Residency. They currently facilitate Toolkits: Digital Storytelling with Express Media. Find them @thearieszone on Instagram.

Emma Jane Grey is a Melbourne-based short-form writer of poetry, book reviews, blog posts and more. Emma lives with chronic illness and disability and often draws on these experiences in her writing. You can find Emma talking about books on Instagram @emma_jane_reads.

Keren Heenan has won a number of Australian short-story awards, placed second in the Fish prize and was a winner of the *Griffith Review* Novella Project 2019. Keren is published in Australian journals and anthologies, and in anthologies and online in the US, UK and Ireland.

Suzanne Hermanoczki is a writer, creative-writing teacher and academic currently based in Naarm/Melbourne. She received her first creative writing degree from the University of Hong Kong, and holds a PhD and a Master's degree in Creative Writing from the University of Melbourne. She is co-founder of Writing Days.

Will Hunt is Assistant Editor at *Australian Book Review*.

Taylor Johnson is a Melbourne-based fiction writer who dabbles in science fiction, post-modernism and humour. His grandmother thinks he's a star but doesn't quite understand what he means when he says 'writing' is his hobby. His work has previously been published in The Dante Aligheri Society of Canberra monthly newsletter.

Henry Johnston is a novelist. He writes short stories, essays and poems. He contributes to *Independent Australia*. His career included roles as an ABC radio producer, a speechwriter, and a senior policy advisor for the NSW government.

Sharon Kernot is an Adelaide-based writer of fiction and poetry. Her recent publications include two verse novels, *The Art of Taxidermy* and *Birdy*. Her short stories and poems have been published widely in Australia and overseas.

Joshua Klarica recently received the MPhil in English Studies from Cambridge. Back home, he lives and works on Gadigal and Wangal land, where he writes poetry and prose. He has had work published in *Meanjin*, *Literary Review*, *Griffith Review* and *Overland Literary Journal*.

Poetry is a way **Edward Kus** punctuates his life: clarifying and expressing its colour and perspective, and building breathing spaces in the rushes. Ed is a father, husband, lawyer and poet based in Naarm/Melbourne, Australia. Poetry helps him to glimpse and articulate his experience that is all those multitudes combined.

Mike Ladd is a poet and essayist. His most recent book is *Dream Tetras* (2022), an experimental collaboration with visual artist Cathy Brooks. Mike was the editor of ABC Radio National's *Poetica* program, which ran for eighteen years and brought Australian and international poetry to a wide audience.

Allan Lake's latest chapbook of poems, *My Photos of Sicily*, was published by Ginninderra Press. Such journals as *The Hong Kong Review*, *Quadrant Magazine*, *The American Writers Review*, *Tokyo Poetry Journal*, *The Antigonish Review*, *New Philosopher* and *The Fabians Review* have published his poems.

Rozanna Lilley's scholarly research, essays and poems are widely published, including in *Best Australian Essays* (2013 and 2014) and *Best of Australian Poems* (2015 and 2023). Her hybrid prose-poetry memoir *Do Oysters Get Bored?: A Curious Life* (UWA Publishing, 2018) was shortlisted for the National Biography Award in 2019. Her poetry chapbook, *The Lady in the Bottle* (Black Spring Press), was released in 2023. For more details see https://rozannalilley.com.au

Rowena Lennox is the author of numerous essays, stories and poems, as well as research on dingoes, and two books: *Dingo Bold*, about dingoes on K'gari/Fraser Island, and *Fighting Spirit of East Timor*, a biography of an East Timorese church leader. She teaches creative writing and lives on Gweagal Country. For more, see rowenalennox.com

Hannah McCann is an academic and writer living in Naarm/Melbourne. She has published/forthcoming poetry in *Westerly Magazine*, *Meniscus Literary Journal*, *DUST* and elsewhere.

Anna McHugh was born in Scotland and came to Australia in 1995. She did a PhD at the University of Sydney, and a DPhil and post-doctoral fellowship at Oxford. She returned to Sydney and was an unsuccessful school teacher. She is now a successful dog-walker.

Brendon IJ McLeod is studying a PhD in English and Writing at the University of Sydney. His poem 'split mind' was shortlisted for the 2023 Overland Judith Wright Poetry Prize and his unpublished novel 'The Rhinoceros' was awarded a fellowship from The Writers' Space to Varuna, the National Writers' House. His work appears or is forthcoming in *Rabbit Poetry*, *Overland* and other venues. He lives and works gratefully on Wiradyuri Country.

Isabella G Mead's debut poetry collection, *The Infant Vine*, was published in 2024 by UWAP. Her work has also appeared in *Meanjin*, *Island*, *Rabbit*, *Westerly*, *Cordite* and *Anthropocene*. In 2024, she won the Venie Holmgren Environmental Poetry Prize. She lives, writes and raises her young family on unceded Wurundjeri land.

Gina Mercer grew up on Bundjalung Country, where her mother immersed her in the joy of word play. This gifted Gina a career working with words—as writer, editor, teacher. She's published thirteen books—from academic work to feminist fiction to elemental and eclectic poetry (the latest is *Watermark*, Ginninderra Press).

Lauren Mitchell is a storyteller from the Victorian goldfields. She has worked as a journalist, magazine editor, digital producer and in corporate communications. She is the author of eight books and has written extensively on the arts, architecture, education and health.

Scott-Patrick Mitchell is a WA-based queer non-binary poet who was the recipient of 2022's Red Room Poetry Fellowship and *Westerly*'s 2022 Mid-Career Fellowship. Their debut poetry collection *Clean* (Upswell Publishing, 2022) was shortlisted for the Prime Minister's Literary Awards, the WA Premier's Book Awards and the Victorian Premier's Literary Awards.

Mark O'Flynn has published seven collections of poetry, most recently *Undercoat* (Liquid Amber Press, 2022) and *Einstein's Brain* (Puncher & Wattmann, 2022). His novels include *The Last Days of Ava Langdon* (UQP), *Grassdogs* (Harper Collins) and *The Forgotten World* (HC).

Kate O'Neil writes for children and adults and has been published in magazines and anthologies in Australia, NZ and the UK: *The Caterpillar*, *The School Magazine NSW*, Emma Press anthologies, *Grieve*, *Poetica Christi*, *Heroines*, *Telling Australia's Truth*, *Chroma* (SCWC), *Azuria* (Geelong) etc.

Born in the Netherlands, **Paul van der Plank** moved with his family to the Australian bush. He is married with two grown-up children. Writing is an essential part of a life comprising CFA call-outs, watching films and soccer, reading Dutch and English literature and activities essential to survival in the bush.

Sandra Renew's latest collection is *She Goes to Town* (Life before Man/ Gazebo Books, 2024). Sandra's poetry has been awarded two Canberra Critics Circle Awards and her collection *It's the Sugar, Sugar* (Recent Work Press, 2021) won a 2021 ACT Notable Poetry Award.

Paris Rosemont is an Asian-Australian poet and author of poetry collections *Banana Girl* and *Barefoot Poetess* (WestWords). Her debut was shortlisted for poetry book awards in Australia, Greece and the UK, and awarded 'Distinguished Favorite' in the NYC Independent Press Award. Paris may be found on Instagram @msparisrose.

Autumn Royal creates drama, poetry and criticism. Since 2016, Autumn has been the interviews editor at *Cordite Poetry Review.*

Pat Saunders is from Perth, Western Australia, and was a runner-up in the 2024 Sejong International Sijo Competition. Her poetry appears in *Catchment: Poetry of Place*, *Verge* and *redrosethorns*, and her short fiction in the anthologies *The Heart Will Find a Way*, *Voices of the South*, *witcraft 24* and *Yah! All Queer.*

Cameron Semmens is an Australian poet and counsellor. He was a finalist of the Newcastle Poetry Prize (2017) and the winner of the Woorilla Poetry Prize (2015). He has published twenty-seven books of poetry, released six spoken-word albums and curates two poetry podcasts: *Shards* and *The Persian and the Poet.*

Ann Shenfield works across various media. Her poetry has received numerous honours including the Judith Wright Poetry Prize and the Rosemary Dobson Prize. Her poetry book *A Treatment* (Upswell Publishing) was listed in *The Age* Best Books of 2023. Last year she completed a four-year program at the Australian Centre for Psychoanalysis in clinical and theoretical studies.

Stephen Smithyman has published two poetry collections, *Snapshot in the Dark* (2018) and *Halfway and Back* (2020) with Ginninderra Press, Adelaide. 'New Year's Day, 1969' is included in his new collection, *Reading 'Anna Karenina' on the Beach*, which is due out from Melbourne Poets Union later this year.

Amelia Theodorakis is a writer from Melbourne/Naarm. Her work has appeared in *Cordite Poetry Review*, *Meanjin Quarterly*, *Australian Poetry Journal* and *The Saturday Paper*, among others.